Tai

John J. Metzler

Taiwan's Transformation

1895 to the Present

John J. Metzler
St. John's University
Jamaica, USA

ISBN 978-1-137-57492-3   ISBN 978-1-137-56442-9 (eBook)
DOI 10.1057/978-1-137-56442-9

Library of Congress Control Number: 2016950469

© The Editor(s) (if applicable) and The Author(s) 2017
This work is subject to copyright. All rights are solely and exclusively licensed by the Publisher, whether the whole or part of the material is concerned, specifically the rights of translation, reprinting, reuse of illustrations, recitation, broadcasting, reproduction on microfilms or in any other physical way, and transmission or information storage and retrieval, electronic adaptation, computer software, or by similar or dissimilar methodology now known or hereafter developed.
The use of general descriptive names, registered names, trademarks, service marks, etc. in this publication does not imply, even in the absence of a specific statement, that such names are exempt from the relevant protective laws and regulations and therefore free for general use.
The publisher, the authors and the editors are safe to assume that the advice and information in this book are believed to be true and accurate at the date of publication. Neither the publisher nor the authors or the editors give a warranty, express or implied, with respect to the material contained herein or for any errors or omissions that may have been made.

Cover illustration: © Sean Pavone / Alamy Stock Photo

Printed on acid-free paper

This Palgrave Macmillan imprint is published by Springer Nature
The registered company is Nature America Inc.
The registered company address is: 1 New York Plaza, New York, NY 10004, U.S.A.

Preface

Taiwan's Transformation 1895–2015: Explaining the Miracle

Today's Taiwan is usually described in superlatives: Dynamic, Entrepreneurial, Prosperous, Vibrant, and, most of all, the enduring East Asian Miracle. But it was not always that way. Miracles just do not happen, they need to be visualized, planned, nurtured, and encouraged. Politicians need to govern, not to rule. Business needs incentives and encouragement, but especially freedom. Societies need security, both military and social. Stability then follows.

Since the 1980s, Taiwan has primarily been viewed as a thriving economic model.

Though certainly true, this assessment belies the amazing social and political success story for 23 million people on a small New Hampshire-sized island just off the China coast. Taiwan's legendary socio-economic miracle has created, inadvertently or not, the island's thriving democracy. Taiwan's freedom emerged in part because its people were better educated, more prosperous, and part of a peaceful revolution of expectations.

If we were to use the broad brush strokes of a Chinese calligrapher, one could almost describe the island's political evolution as a reflection of Seymour Martin Lipset's modernization theory through which economic development and industrialization nurture democracy. And that democracy is reinforced by an entrenched middle class.

Taiwan remains a place of glaring contrasts too. The superlative National Palace Museum remains a proud repository of 5000 years of

Chinese history, and the Taipei 101 skyscraper offers a futuristic architecture and stands as one of the world's tallest buildings.

Taiwan has its own terminology too, a lexicon of Chinese studies which I try to keep to a rhetorical minimum. The government official nomenclature, changing and evolving since 1949, is reflected in the actual chapter titles from the formal Republic of China to the Taiwan (Republic of China) of the Democratic Progressive Party era to the current Taiwan/Republic of China. Each period and era are marked by the changing nuance of politics. This is not likely to change.

Yet, in almost direct proportion to Taiwan's marked success has been Mainland China's expanding economy, its more assertive military postures, and indeed the island's still unresolved status as a "renegade" province to be returned to the Chinese "motherland."

Waiting for a flight to Taiwan, I overheard a simple conversation between an airport worker and some other waiting passengers in New York. When the worker casually asked a family where their flight was heading, they replied, "To Taiwan." Slightly bemused, the employee asked as if almost in jest, "Is Taiwan a suburb of China?" While my initial instinct beyond disbelief was "do you know your geography?" or "do you read newspapers?" I then realized that 20 years ago some students may have said, "Made in Taiwan—is that some major manufacturer?"

Taiwan has been less threatened by Beijing in recent years as much as being overshadowed and possibly absorbed by it. Add a healthy dose of Beijing *soft power* diplomacy, and Taiwan's noteworthy narrative is gradually being airbrushed out of the picture.

But notwithstanding the geopolitical force from China, Taiwan's vibrant democracy equally poses a *poignant philosophical challenge* to the Mainland.

Yet, Taiwan, the "other China" if you will, no longer follows the expected political template. Though a thriving and prosperous democracy, Taiwan's major trading partner is the People's Republic of China, its primary political antagonist. Moreover, Mainland China and Taiwan, despite their formal political ostracism, maintain vibrant commercial, economic, and tourist ties.

Taiwan's status, its de facto sovereignty and political freedoms, is slowly becoming shadowed, some would say *Finlandized*; this became especially apparent in Ma Ying-jeou's second term.

How the new DPP government will seriously alter this course shall set the political agenda for the post-2016 era.

John J. Metzler
Jamaica, NY

Contents

1. Japanese Interlude 1895–1945 — 1
2. Return to Chinese Rule 1945–1950 — 21
3. Free China; Cold War Fortress 1951–1971 — 39
4. The Republic of China 1972–1992 — 59
5. The Republic of China on Taiwan 1993–1999 — 79
6. Taiwan (The Republic of China) 2000–2008 — 93
7. Taiwan/Republic of China 2008–2016 — 111
8. Conclusions: Prospects and Portents — 137

Annex — 149

Bibliography 167

Index 171

List of Maps and Photos

Maps

Map 1	Taiwan	150
Map 2	Taiwan Straits	151

Photos

Photo 1   Kaohsiung city and harbor. The southern city of Kaohsiung remains Taiwan major port city and is in fact one of Asia's largest container ports 152

Photo 2   Downtown Taipei traffic. Taiwan's society has evolved from motorbikes to cars in recent decades. Taipei has become an increasingly "green" and "wired" city 152

Photo 3   Taiwan Old and New. Reflection from a temple on the glass of a modern building 153

List of Tables

Table A1 Countries with which the ROC/Taiwan maintains full
          diplomatic relations: 22   155
Table A2 Taiwan de facto overseas representation (select examples)   155
Table A3 Taiwan economic growth rates and per capita incomes
          (select years)   160
Table A4 Mainland Chinese visitors to Taiwan (select monthly statistics) 160
Table A5 China/Taiwan contact chart form 1955 to 2016   165

CHAPTER 1

Japanese Interlude 1895–1945

INTRODUCTION

Known as *Ilha Formosa* by Portuguese mariners, later settled by the Dutch, and then emerging as a Ming loyalist stronghold after collapse of China's most brilliant Dynasty, the island of Taiwan was long coveted for its geography, being both on the doorstep of China and on the crossroads of East Asian commerce.

By the nineteenth century, the island assumed new prominence as Western powers ambitiously and methodically encroached upon Qing China's sovereignty. The Opium War saw a British victory which soon translated into Queen Victoria's Empire extending into a string of Treaty Ports on the China coast ranging from Shanghai and Ningpo in the north, Amoy and Foochow in the center, to Hong Kong in the south. The French, not to be outdone, and after a short but sharp conflict with China in 1884, would gain a foothold in Taiwan's ports of Keelung and Tainan as well as the Pescadores Islands in the Taiwan Strait. Equally, France, along with many other European powers, had "concession rights" in the important city of Shanghai.

Not far away in Japan, an American naval squadron led by Commodore Matthew Perry had arrived in Tokyo Bay. Perry's formidable steam-powered "Black Ships" were viewed by the Japanese as "giant dragons puffing smoke" sent to pry open the doors of commerce in a closed and insulated Japan. The ruling Tokugawa *shogunate*, fully aware of what had transpired across the sea in China after the Opium War and nervous over

© The Editor(s) (if applicable) and The Author(s) 2017
J.J. Metzler, *Taiwan's Transformation*,
DOI 10.1057/978-1-137-56442-9_1

their own vulnerability to the powerful guns on the US Navy ships, concluded that it was better to deal with the distant barbarians than to try to oppose them, at least for the time being. Treaties of Peace and Friendship were later signed between the Americans and Japan's rulers in 1854 and 1858, opening additional trading ports, which would set the template for Washington's relations with the still isolated Japan.

The China coast was being carved up into "concessions" where the European powers would gain commercial access to markets, opportunities for missionary activities, all backed up by unapologetic gunboat diplomacy. By the early 1890s, the map of China was nearly spoken for; the European powers had taken what they wanted.

Across the waters in Japan, an extraordinary political event had occurred in 1868. The Meiji Restoration had toppled the old Tokugawa military *shogunate*, forcibly united over 300 small feudal fiefdoms, had reinstated the Emperor and thus Imperial rule, and as importantly had set a modernizing path for the Land of the Rising Sun. Modernization, "westernization," and a zealous desire to learn from and to imitate the West would soon put Japan on a trajectory to success. Meiji's modernization had many positive aspects, which saw the once isolated country transform itself from a staid island nation into a late-nineteenth-century powerhouse.

Meiji's meteoric rise in Japan's socio-economic situation equally saw the new government seeking foreign political models and systems from which to borrow. The government's missions ventured abroad to Britain, France, Germany, and the USA to get a firsthand experience of how foreign governmental and constitutional systems worked. Before long, the study missions concluded that Prussia's constitution would be best suited to Japan.

Contrary to China's Qing Dynasty, and its rather more timid and reserved Self-Strengthening Movement, the Japanese embraced Westernization, especially its technology, industrialization, and universal public educational standards. Military modernization was not far behind and the old post-Perry slogan "Respect the Emperor, expel the barbarians" took on a new meaning.

Meiji's modernizers also, according to Ian Buruma, "Managed to pick some of the worst, most bellicose aspects of the Western world for emulation in Japan. One of them was colonialism." Honda Toshiaki, one of the more prominent reformers who was particularly enchanted with Great Britain, argued that without a colonial empire, a nation could not achieve greatness. "His visions of Japan's colonial enterprise were, like his politics, both progressive and ruthless, rather like his favorite model Britain," states

Buruma. Honda's philosophy exhibited the dualistic paternalism which would soon descend upon Formosa. "It is the task of the ruler-father to direct and educate the natives in such a manner that there will not be a single one of them who spends even one unproductive day."[1]

The Meiji court, which had moved from the ancient city of Kyoto to the new imperial capital Edo (Tokyo), was smitten by the powers of the West as well as its creature comforts and cultural mores. Japanese would dress in Western clothing, eat Western food, dance to the tunes of the day, and display the benefits of the modern era. Unknown to many, Edo was already a thriving metropolis with a population larger than London or New York.

Japan would now showcase to Asia and the world what and how fast they were learning.

The famed woodblock *Ukiyo-e* prints, through which Japan graphically portrayed its samurai heroes, courtesans, and Kabuki plays through stunning color and detail were gradually replaced with such themes as modern city life with street scenes clogged with a maze of electric and telegraph lines, trolley cars, and strolling couples in overstated nineteenth-century garb. By 1895, the woodblocks would chronicle the saga of Japan's war with China, and a decade after that in 1905, they would reflect the hyper-patriotism of the Russo-Japanese War. Woodblock prints made the General Staff look distinctly Prussian in uniforms and demeanor. The Japanese were becoming comfortable with their role as a "modern country" as importantly with their national status.

Set in the political geography of the Pacific in the mid-1890s, Japan remained the anxious onlooker. Great Britain, France, and the Netherlands all had staked their claims from Malaya, the Dutch East Indies, and Indochina in the south to a string of port concessions on the China coast. Spain controlled the Philippine islands. Qing China held political sway on the Korean peninsula. Russia, through its controlling interests in the Manchurian railroads and ties to the Korean kingdom, was equally a regional player.

"By the end of the 19th century, East Asia had become a stage of imperial competition among the great powers. With regards to the Korean peninsula, Japan, Ching (Qing) China, and Russia waged a fierce competition to place the weak kingdom under their control," writes Seung-young Kim. He adds, "Though a declining empire, China (Qing) tried to strengthen its traditional suzerainty over Korea. Japan had regarded Korea as a 'dagger against the heart of Japan,' and constantly tried to strengthen its influence on the peninsula. Russia also tried to secure ice-free ports on the Korean coast and its construction of the trans-Siberian railroad made Japan worry about the future threat from Russia," adds Prof. Kim.[2]

The Sino-Japanese War of 1894–1895 largely reflected Japan's strategic desire to pull Korea from a near millennium of Chinese influence and into the grip of a militarily and economically ascendant Japan. Yet as Kim opines, "But the broader origin of the war had to do with the construction of the trans-Siberian railroad which began in May 1891. Japan had already been regarding Russia as its primary enemy. … In this context, a war against China was to a certain degree a preemptive move by Japan to prepare for the coming confrontation with Russia."[3]

Japan's Colonial Temptations

Objectively speaking, the Sino-Japanese War created a new political order in East Asia and, importantly, created new positive perceptions of Meiji Japan. "A new balance of power had emerged. China's millennia-long unquestioned dominance had abruptly ended. Japan was on the rise with momentous consequences in store for the East and the West," writes Prof. S. C. M. Paine of the US Naval War College. "The Western perception of Japan as a great power was born in September of 1894. Over a three-day period, Japan used modern arms so professionally and defeated China on land and sea so decisively, that quite suddenly the Western world perceived Japan as a modern power. … If this first Sino/Japanese War catapulted Japan into the ranks of the powers, it hurtled China on a long downward spiral," adds Prof. Paine.[4]

In a series of land and sea battles across the Korean peninsula in 1894, the Japanese conclusively defeated the Qing Chinese forces and as importantly sealed the fate of Korea for the next half century. Stunningly, the fall of Port Arthur on the Liaodong Peninsula brought Japanese forces into Mainland China proper and dangerously close to the Qing Imperial capital at Peking. Again, Japan's popular media expressed in colorful if exaggerated views of the *Ukiyo-e* prints, extolled hyper-patriotism which would serve as a political narcotic for the next decade and then again in the 1930s.

The final act of the war would be staged in Shimonoseki, a small Japanese port facing Korea. Here, the Imperial Chinese delegation led by Viceroy Li Hung Chang would spar for peace terms with the legendary Meiji reformer Count Ito Hirobumi. In March and April of 1895, the two East Asian powers, Qing China and Meiji Japan would debate peace and discuss its terms in a draft treaty.

We are reminded that the Japanese Navy wanted access to Taiwan while the Army demanded the Liaodong Peninsula. "Premier Ito was a great admirer of Otto von Bismarck. He hoped to emulate Germany's victory over France in the Franco Prussian war of 1870–71. That war had served to both unify Germany internally and to raise its prestige internationally," writes Paine. Importantly, "Just as Ito has modeled the Meiji Constitution on that of Prussia, so he wanted the Treaty of Shimonoseki to mirror key features of the 1871 Treaty of Frankfurt; territorial annexation, a large indemnity, occupation of an enemy city to ensure payment of the indemnity, and so on."[5]

The Treaty of Shimonoseki was worded in the flowery nineteenth-century diplomatic prose of the era: "His Majesty the Emperor of China and His Majesty the Emperor of Japan desiring to restore the blessings of peace to the countries and subjects and to remove all cause for future complications," have agreed to the following articles; Article 1 "China recognizes definitely the full and complete independence and autonomy of Corea." Article 2 "China cedes to Japan in perpetuity and full sovereignty of the following territories together with their fortifications. ... The island of Formosa, together with all the islands appertaining or belonging to the said island of Formosa." Japan equally would gain the strategic Liaodong Peninsula. Eleven other articles would further serve to codify Qing China's humiliation. On 17 April 1895, Viceroy Li Hung Chang signed for China and Count Ito Hirobumi for Japan.[6]

Thus, in the 28 years of Meiji rule, Japan had forced itself onto the East Asian stage as a regional power. But Tokyo had pushed too far. Less than a week after the signing of the Treaty, Ministers of Russia, Germany, and France called on the Japanese Foreign Ministry to offer some "friendly advice." They recommended that Japan return the Liaodong Peninsula to China. What became known as the *Triple Intervention* by the European powers put a damper on Japan's regional designs for the next decade. In November of the same year, Viceroy Li Hung Chang presided over the return of Liaodong to China but with a further indemnity to Japan.[7]

While the Western European powers were not necessarily opposed to Japan taking some East Asian spoils, it became abundantly clear that the same powers were not going to let Japan pick its territorial claims *carte blanche* in any way which may remotely impinge upon European plans, perceptions, or desires. Part of the "friendly advice" from Russia, Germany, and France came in the form of warships to help Japan come to a decision.

Consequently, Japan's plan to hold the Liaodong Peninsula in China was viewed by Russia, Germany, and France as getting just a bit too close for strategic comfort. After all, Meiji Japan was hardly a full-fledged member of the "club" and would have to accept its associate status until such a time as the other powers could enforce it.

China's young Emperor Guangxu, barely out of the shadows of the Dowager Empress, was as politically tarnished by having his diplomatic plenipotentiary place the Imperial Seal on the Treaty as by the unremarkable performance of the Chinese troops in battle against Japan.

Shortly after signing the Treaty of Shimonoseki, the US Secretary of the Navy Hilary Herbert wrote, "Japan has leaped, almost at one bound, to a place among the great nations of the earth. Her recent exploits in the war in China have focused all eyes upon her."[8]

Lafcadio Hearn, an American author living in Japan, expounded, "the real birthday of New Japan, began with the conquest of China."[9]

Formosa

Ilha Formosa, or beautiful island, as named by Portuguese mariners in the 1500s, had been under the sway of the Dutch, Ming Chinese loyalists attempting to use this offshore island as a springboard to re-conquer the Mainland, and various buccaneers. But it was during the Qing Dynasty that the Emperor Kangxsi brought Formosa under Chinese control as part of neighboring Fukien Province.

A score of Malay Polonesian aborigine tribes inhabited the mountainous interior while the Chinese, mostly migrants from coastal Fukien Province, lived in the lowlands and towns. US Commodore Perry of Japan fame had recommended a joint Sino-American economic development program with an American settlement in Keelung; others considered purchasing the island from China. This tropical island frontier region, though being viewed apprehensively by many onlookers, was equally tempting to others.

As recently as 1884, the French had seized the Formosa Straits and established a foothold in the northern port of Keelung. Only in 1887 was Formosa detached from coastal Fukien Province and declared a new Province of the Great Qing Empire.

The appointment of Liu Ming-ch'uan as Governor a decade before Japan seized control of the island brought about a vigorous, if short, economic and social vitalization of Formosa.

Governor Liu set about an ambitious program to make Formosa, really a maritime frontier province, into a thriving part of the Great Qing Empire. The Governor fostered building a railroad, postal, and telegraph lines and established steamship and cable connections overseas. Indeed he built the comparatively modern capital city, Taipei, and, according to onlookers, "Formosa was beyond doubt the most progressive province on all of China." According to historian George H. Kerr, "Liu's comparatively great success could be attributed in part to the pact that he was working with an island people less tradition-bound than the Chinese masses on the continent. They were frontiersmen and pioneers by tradition, obliged to experiment in new situations ... they were beginning to look away from the continent to a world beyond China." Kerr adds, "Between 1870 and 1890 there had been spectacular economic growth, bringing a harvest of silver dollars into Formosan hands."[10]

Many narratives of nineteenth-century Formosa relate the tired tale of an impoverished tropical island with tenuous links to Peking. The modernization saga commences with the arrival of the Japanese and the purported transformation of sleepy Formosa into an increasingly prosperous colonial outpost of the Empire of the Sun. This was not really the case.

Governor Liu's plans were revolutionary in the context of late Qing China. He would transform the island into a "modern progressive Confucian state ... he would adopt the modern ideas and methods of Western science and industry within the framework of Confucianism," opines W.G. Goddard. After travels all over the island to see for himself the reality and the challenges which confronted him, Governor Liu decided that "Taipei was to be the symbol of the new China. Not vast palaces, roofed with ornate and richly colored porcelain tiles ... rather a city throbbing with modernity, from which would radiate the spirit of progress." In 1887, the Governor turned on the first electric lights in Taipei, making the capital the first city in the Chinese world to be electrified. He stressed on transport and railways. Despite the tough terrain, a rail line was built from Taipei to Keelung in 1889. A school for telegraph operations was set up in the capital.[11]

Turning to commerce, Governor Liu developed the island's legendary resources: camphor, wood, and tea. The storied Oolong tea harvested under strict standards and plantations was allowed for export. Production increased to 20 million pounds by the end of his tenure. He stressed education but not in bowing deference to the West as much as a synthesis of the best of the Western where a modern state was guided by individuals steeped in the Confucian ethic. Goddard described Liu's "Formosa as a modern state, applying the latest scientific methods of the West, yet retaining its ancient Confucian foundation." Liu's "modernizing ideas," were nonetheless viewed as dangerous by the ultraconservative Confucians in the Qing capital Peking. The Governor was recalled in 1891.[12]

Formosa was long defined for its commercial instincts; even in the Qing Dynasty, the island emerged as a producer of sugar, tea, and camphor. By the 1870s, tea had become the island's green gold. As Americans developed a taste for "Formosa Oolong" the cultivation, processing, and trading defined a lucrative agricultural industry. Taiwan's tea trade relied upon the capitalization of foreign and mainland Chinese banks. Agencies or branches of major Western exchange banks extended loans to foreign exporters," advises Robert Gardella. In fact, given the large American demand for the green gold, annual "exports increased a hundredfold from the mid 1860s to the late 1880s; from 185,000 lbs. to 18–20 million pounds." He adds, "Formosa tea offered an initial demonstration of Taiwan's subsequent capacity to realize rapid gains from international trade."[13]

The ink and official seals on the Treaty of Shimonoseki had barely dried when in May 1895 the Chinese Governor of Formosa Tang Ching-sung had proclaimed the island an independent republic, "*Taiwan Min-chu Kuo.*" The Declaration of Independence of the Republic of Taiwan stated: "The Japanese have insulted China by annexing our territory of Taiwan. The People of Taiwan, in vain, have appealed to the Throne. Now the Japanese are about to arrive." Importantly, President Tang stated, "The Republic of Taiwan and stands in the relation of a tributary state of China" and recognizes the suzerainty of the Emperor of China. Interestingly, this young Republic was forged not by arms and warlords but by the *literati,* a government of writers, philosophers, and Confucian scholars. The spirit of the young Formosan Republic was soon swamped by the force of arms from Japan.[14]

Despite the almost immediate setbacks, the young republic reflected both a virulent nationalism and a desire to pursue a more socially progressive path than that being followed in Manchu China.

Between June and October, Taiwan's resistance was subdued by Japan's elite Household Guards Division. But during the campaign from Keelung in the north to Tainan in the south, the Guards suffered an astounding 32,000 casualties, mostly resulting from the horrible tropical conditions; 164 killed in action and 515 wounded were surpassed by over 4600 deaths from disease, with a further 27,000 men sent home as unfit for service. Nonetheless, Japan now had control over three million new subjects. Given Formosa's role as Japan's first colony, the island was a special preserve of the military. Formosa would be governed by Admirals and Generals from 1895 to 1919, and again from 1936 to 1945. Those civil governors in between were experienced in police administration at the prefectural and national levels. Though the administrative machinery was clearly security oriented, the new colony equally attracted young university graduates and administrators who would test new theories and techniques in this colony.[15]

Model Tropical Colony

A Bureau of Industry was established to facilitate economic planning. The first Director was Dr. Nitobe Inazo, a young man from Hokkaido who had studied both at the American-established Sapporo Agricultural College and later at Johns Hopkins University in Baltimore, Maryland, where he became an associate of Woodrow Wilson and John Dewey. Dr. Nitobe, who later converted to Christianity, epitomized the young, Western-educated, civilian class of technocrats who would form the cornerstone of Japan's colonial experiment.

The rich soil and tropical forests made Formosa an extraordinary proving ground for Japan's progressive agricultural plans but equally a productive new outpost for its wider imperial projects. Despite the enthusiasm of Dr. Nitobe's compatriots, the early Japanese administration was befuddled by language barriers, cultural misunderstandings, and the obstinacy of Formosans. The training of translators, interpreters, and technicians who would fan out throughout the island, almost always accompanied by fellow Japanese constables and gendarmes, posed a unique practical hurdle. As Kerr asserts, "Dr. Nitobe's elaborate plans constituted a broad attack upon the entire traditional structure of Formosan community life."[16]

The Japanese occupation of Formosa represented the first significant steps to make the Empire of the Sun a rising colonial power. Nonetheless, Meiji's deference to Western science and socio-political norms had created a sense of inferiority among many Japanese. As Goddard opines, "Out of this sense of national inferiority, first to China and then to the West, was born a megalomania which saw Japan as the divine country, to which all others would bow the knee, and from which a new civilization, a synthesis of Japanese culture and Western technology would spread throughout the seven seas."[17]

In parallel to Japan's actions, the European and American were expanding their influence in East Asian waters. Just three years after the Treaty of Shimonoseki, placing Formosa under Tokyo's tutelage, Admiral George Dewey entered Manila Bay and defeated the Spanish fleet. The Philippines came under American control in 1898 as did Guam and Hawaii farther afield. Germany moreover carved out its niche on the China coast in Klaichow in Shantung Province. The coastal map and offshore islands sprouted foreign flags. Equally, on the vast landmass to the north Russia was flexing its muscles. Japan noted these geopolitical shifts with apprehension as well as the smug satisfaction in being a member of the same colonial club.

The Japanese Governor-General Kodama Gentaro, Civil Administrator Dr. Goto Shimpei, and the able Dr. Nitobe unrolled a master plan for Taipei which reflected both the zeal for progressive change and the desire to copy the grand boulevards of Paris. A government quarter, a commercial district, and residential sections for the needs of a projected 600,000 residents were planned. The massive red brick government buildings which stand to this day were built in this period. As Kerr opines, "The ponderous 'Prussian mansard' style of many official buildings reflected Dr. Goto's taste in Western architecture and his distant student days in Berlin. The grid and radial street patterns and the shaded boulevards and parks would dominate the grand plan of Japanese *Taihoku* and later other towns throughout Formosa. Taipei was destined to become a modern colonial capital.[18]

Taipei Meiji Architecture Following Japan's Meiji Restoration in 1868, the island kingdom embraced nearly all things Western from education, science and technology, and military mores to a formal Constitution. Architecture began to mirror the West too with large brick buildings and government offices. Besides Western architecture found in port cities, such as Yokohama, Nagasaki, and Kobe, the style soon appeared in Taiwan. To this day Japan's imperial legacy can be found in Taipei, where large red brick structures ranging from the Presidential building (the former Governor-General's office) which dates to 1906 to a series of other government structures such as the Taipei Guest House, a baroque building reflecting French Second Empire styles built between 1899 and 1900. Other such structures reflect a British influence. The former Taipei headquarters of the Taiwan Tobacco and Liquor Monopoly, the 1914 Huashan Creative Park, has been turned into an arts center free space for individual galleries and boutiques. Much of the Meiji period architecture in Taipei was directed by Morinosuke Matsuyama who became the construction chief for the Japanese Governor-General's Office in 1906.

Source: American Chamber of Commerce/Taipei "Taipei Area: Colonial-era Japanese Buildings Project European Style," by Philip Liu.

Public health issues were the special purview of Dr. Goto, himself a medical doctor, who quickly understood the dangers of the festering disease potential in Formosa's sub-tropical climate. Health, hygiene, and medical services were initiated. By 1898, public hospital and medical college were established in the capital. Japan's moves toward public health and disease control looked remarkably similar to America's own endeavors in Panama a decade later.

But beyond progressive public health improvements for the population, there was a darker side to taking care of the populace. Dr. Goto revived the ancient *hoko* registration system in 1898. Formosans were required to partake in this household registration system through which the Japanese could exert control. By 1903, the Japanese had registered over 500,000 households; the system, involving a web of control and obligation, would last until 1945. The Youth Corps was also established to bring young men under scrutiny and offer them responsibilities and privileges in direct proportion to their cooperation with the colonial authorities. The Youth Corps was engaged in firefighting, road maintenance, and passive security duties. By 1903, its membership stood at 55,000 and grew steadily.[19]

The Bank of Taiwan was established in 1899. The bank inherited a complicated and arcane system from the Chinese rule where foreign-milled silver coins from Mexico and South America were often used along with strings of copper coins. Within a decade, the Japanese had instituted a decimal system coinage and paper, a currency which would become obligatory.

As George Kerr relates approvingly, "Kodama, Goto and Nitobe undoubtedly set Formosa on the road to an unprecedented prosperity. Although it was obvious from the beginning that a disproportionate share of the profit went off to Japan proper, every Formosan shared to some degree in rising living standards; roads, railroads, telegraph lines, post offices school hospitals."[20]

The Japanese expanded railroads and port facilities. At the time of Japan's occupation of Formosa, there was a 62-mile (100 kilometers) rail line from the port of Keelung. By the mid-1930s, total rail track was over 880 kilometers.[21]

The Japanese could toast their success with the establishment in 1916 of a winery at Huashan which produced *sake* and ginseng wines. A few years after, the government established the Taiwan Governor-General's Monopoly Bureau—Taipei Wine Factory.[22]

Interestingly, besides sake, salt, camphor, tobacco, and opium were placed under the monopoly. Upon their arrival in 1895, the Japanese discovered many opium addicts in Formosa. The Japanese instituted a tightly controlled manufacture, distribution, and registry of opium users throughout Taiwan. In September 1900, some 169,000 names were registered for which licenses were granted. By 1932, users had officially dropped to 19,550. Sales of the drug declined dramatically too from 87 million grams in 1906 down to 21 million grams in 1933. Tokyo was particularly proud to say that her policies were in conformity with the League of Nations International Opium Treaty.[23]

Tokyo's hubris often frothed over in describing the Taiwan escapade. In the book *"The Development of Colonial Taiwan," from 1916*, we see, "We have admirably transformed this chaotic situation, restored peace, established order, realized financial independence, attended to the development of natural resources, promoted industrialization, and secured the livelihoods and properties of the people on the island. ... The reason for our distinguished record in colonization is the result of the Japanese race's unique ability to rule another people and our skill in colonial management. It also speaks to the grand efficacy of managing a tropical colony."[24]

Takekoshi Yosaburu, a Parliamentarian and journalist, proudly proclaimed, "Japan can point to her success thus far in Formosa as a proof of her worthiness to be admitted into the community of the world's great colonial powers." He added, "I cannot help but rejoice that we, the Japanese, have passed our first examination as a colonizing nation so creditably ... our success in Formosa beckon us on to fulfill the great destiny that lies before us, and to make our country 'Queen of the Pacific.'" Some American authors of the day reflected this optimism by adding that Japan's achievements were the "exact counterpart of what the United States has done in the Philippine islands."[25]

Another astute observer of Japan's role in Taiwan was none other than Sun Yat-sen, the southern Chinese medical doctor and exiled political activist who was plotting to overthrow the Qing Dynasty. In September 1900, after the celebrated and bungled attempt by Qing operatives to capture him during his time in the British capital, Sun had returned to Japan. Subsequently, he journeyed to Taihoku, Formosa, where he would spend two months. Despite Sun's wanderings from Honolulu, Hawaii, to the USA and throughout Europe to stoke the fires of the national revolution, Formosa was the place which synthesized his thoughts and focus.

"Formosa was his source of inspiration. ... His two months there put iron in his blood and steeled his spirit so that he was able to rise above all disappointments. ... Formosa saved Sun Yat-sen," writes Goddard. Not only was the revolutionary doctor among fellow Chinese after all, but he took special inspiration from Formosa's strong and activist literati, a class of scholars not so tradition-bound as on the Mainland. "Sun Yat-sen, known to the Chinese as the 'Father of the Republic,' had his spiritual baptism in Formosa," opines Goddard. Shortly after leaving Formosa, Sun began to work on his seminal work *San Min Chu I* (Three Principles of the People).[26]

Despite his spiritual inspiration, Dr. Sun's path was to take another 11 years. Ironically, while in Denver, Colorado, on a fundraising trip for the revolutionary movement, Dr. Sun discovered, to his amazement, while reading the newspaper on 12 October that uprising had begun in far-off Wuchang on 10 October. Leaving the Brown Palace Hotel, Sun Yat-sen was determined to return to China immediately. Sun traveled by train to San Francisco, where he would board a steam ship for China.

Though Taiwan saw its socio-economic integration into the Japanese system, the Emperor never ventured to the island. However, Crown Prince Hirohito visited in April 1923, in a brief sojourn which was laden with ritual and ceremony.

Official Japanese statistics related, "Including the savages, the total population at the end of 1933 in Taiwan was, 5,060,507 ... showing an increase of 130,545 over that at the end of 1932, and 2,023,648 over the end of 1905 when the first census-taking results were announced." The survey adds that there were 4.7 million Taiwan natives, 256,327 Japanese, 43,585 Chinese, and "146,923 aboriginal savages ... the aborigines consist of savages and semi-civilized tribes."[27]

"The Taiwan aborigines are the oldest inhabitants of the island and are classified into semi-civilized aborigines and savage headhunters," according to Tokyo's official verdict. Among the key tribes were the Taiyal, Bunun, Paiwan, and Ami. The report states that "since the occupation of Taiwan to the end of 1933, rifles confiscated numbered 29,772 ... during the 38 years which ended in 1933, over 7,000 people lost their lives at the hands of savages and the largest number of them was 761 in 1912."[28]

Indeed, Taiwanese living in the major cities and towns had begun to accommodate themselves with Japanese rule. A Western observer remarked the urban dwellers were "fast becoming Japanned." They rode bicycles, used the telephone and the post offices, and often wore the wooden Japanese shows. Yet, much of the modernity was but a veneer. In this Japanese colony not bound by the Meiji constitution, "the Taiwan Governor-General continued to reign like a virtual sovereign ... his ventral authority was made to impinge on the Taiwanese, and by 1915, the mountain tribes as well. The Governor-General maintained close surveillance over the Japanese residents, too." Foreign residents, be they Western or Mainland Chinese, were carefully monitored as well.[29]

According to Prof. Harry Lamley,

> "The 1920 reforms also introduced a system of local self-government by which councils were created at the lower levels of government. Between 1920 and 1935, these councils functioned merely as advisory bodies, and their members were appointed by colonial authorities. After further self-government measures were introduced in 1935, the provincial and municipal councils were granted decision making powers, and half the members were elected ... such a limited form of self-rule enabled a few Taiwanese elected (together with leading Japanese residents) to participate marginally in colonial governance and more of the registered population to vote in local elections."[30]

Yet, despite a guise of local government for the Formosans, an interlocking web of local household, village, and civil administration would monitor and serve to assimilate the locals into the Japanese mold. Formosa was being absorbed into Japan's colonial empire on terms Tokyo would control down to the last household. Home-rule for Formosa, as long as it served Japan's political and security template, would be permitted for what many observers were describing as Japan's "Ireland of the East."

Formosa remained restive and occasionally sharply violent. In the high green mountains behind Taichung in the center of the island, the Japanese had established Musha Village, a regional administrative center. On 27 October 1930, at the dedication of a municipal facility by the Governor, aborigines attacked the Japanese gruesomely, killing 197, including the provincial Governor. Retribution was swift and brutal. Japanese military operations killed and captured most of the rebels and their families. Nonetheless, the Musha Rebellion had shocked both Taihoku and Tokyo and reminded authorities that Formosa, while superficially pacified, had deep running resentments, especially among the largely marginalized aborigines.[31]

Japanese views toward Formosa varied; some wanted to view the island as a subordinate region to be held under tight political control and for producing agricultural and raw materials for Japan. Others saw the possibility of assimilating the islanders as Japan had done with the Okinawans.

Kominka, a compromise assimiliation program, offered a workable alternative. *Kominka* stood for complete assimilation, "union with the Emperor's people," or "changing into Imperial subjects." Advocates of the new policy felt that Formosans could "substitute one culture for another throughout the colony." Racial discrimination toward the Formosans was legally scrapped and mixed marriages and social integration were allowed. Both the Japanese and the Formosans would occasionally mix and often adopt Western ways as a cultural compromise. Yet, the *Kominka* program stressed on the symbolism of the Empire of the Sun, as each home was required to have a Shinto shrine altar on which to honor the Sun Goddess and the Emperor Hirohito.[32]

By the 1930s, Formosa boasted a thriving agricultural sector on which rice and sugar production were pillars. Equally, tea cultivation was encouraged with the famous Oolong tea being a key export to the USA and Britain.

The year 1935 was to prove a banner year for Japan's Formosan subjects who would "celebrate" 40 years under Japan's control. Expositions, displays, and conferences were slated to project the progress and harmony of Japan's rule. Previous themes of Agriculture, Industry, and Tropical Industrial research celebrations attracted many visitors from Japan and China, including China's General Chen Yi, Governor of the adjacent coastal province of Fukien. Governor Chen, who was married to a former Japanese geisha, was destined to play a notorious role in Formosa's post-war development.

Equally, Japan allowed the Formosans to elect local government structures in the colony. Though voting was limited to males of at least 25 years of age, nearly 187,000 met the qualifications and over 96 percent voted. Though the assembly system was stacked in favor of the Japanese, the Formosans began to feel a new sense of civic duty and pride. By 1939, over 286,000 Formosans were able to vote in municipal and local elections. Nonetheless, Tokyo refused to allow the concept of an island-wide assembly.

Educational spending for Formosa was surprisingly high; as expected, it focused heavily on primary education. There were over one thousand schools in operation by the time the new Governor Admiral Kobayashi arrived in Taihoku. The reasons were explained by Kerr: "To raise a wall between the oncoming generation and old China, Tokyo was pouring money into the Formosan schools system. Traditional and sentimental ties had to be broken and the Japanese language had to take the place of Chinese dialects." By 1937, more than 500,000 children were in primary schools but a mere 4117 were registered in higher institutions on the island. Commercial colleges and the prestigious Taihoku Imperial University were open to small numbers of Formosans.[33]

Geopolitically, Formosa was evolving into a very different place. As Manchuria has developed into an industrial base and *pseudo-independent* Manchukuo under the patronage of the Imperial Army, so too would Formosa emerge as a southern agricultural bulwark under the control of the Imperial Navy. Both places would serve as springboards for Tokyo's impending aggression into the Chinese Mainland and beyond.

Pacific War Duty

By 1931, Japan had expanded into Manchuria, establishing Manchukuo, a client state which served as a strategic dagger at the heart of China and equally a potential threat to the Soviet Far East. By 1937, Japan formally attacked Nationalist China in the wake of the Marco Polo Bridge incident in July. In this context, Formosa had become a very valuable military chess piece in supporting Tokyo's wider geopolitical moves into Mainland China and Southeast Asia. And, as mentioned, the island's wider industrialization to prepare for supporting this war had started following the 1935 conferences. Now Tokyo would test its subjects.

The *Kominka* imperial policies introduced by Governor-General Kobayashi went from the theoretical to the ruthlessly practical: instituting a national language program to supplant Chinese in 1937, a name-changing kaiseimei plan replacing Chinese names for Japanese ones in 1940. Recruitment for military service soon followed. Equally, State Shinto, Japan's official religion, was strongly promoted at the expense of local Chinese deities and folk religions. Formosans, especially the younger generation who had grown up under the Japanese rule, largely responded positively to military recruitment. Only by 1945, in the desperate last stages of the war, did Japan introduce general conscription. The number of Formosans recruited for duty reached 207,000, including 80,000 servicemen and 127,000 civilian employees. Many Formosan troops served on tropical Hainan island. Equally, widespread elementary education became commonplace; by 1944, three out of four children were in primary school.[34]

Psychological mobilization was stressed for the Formosans. They were drilled to fit into the Japanese military mindset; on a practical level, the islanders ran defense exercises, practiced air raid drills, and participated in patriotic gatherings. Kerr recalls that as part of an "empire-wide spiritual mobilization campaign," and scoolchildren were required to worship at Shinto shrines. He adds, "Formosans remained supremely indifferent to Shinto doctrine. Compulsory attendance on public occasions and the maintenance of a Shinto altar in every house was a nuisance to be borne without protest."[35]

Part of the propaganda culture of the period is reflected in the film *Bell of Sayon*, a 1943 production about the patriotism of villagers in a Taiwan mountain town. An aborigine girl, Sayun Hayun, played by the actress Shirley Yamaguchi, shows her loyalty to Japan.

The film, an adaptation of the hit wartime propaganda song, "Bell of Sayon," underscored Japan's imperial vision for Taiwan.[36]

Admiral Hasegawa Kiyoshi became Formosa's new Governor-General in November 1940. An active member of the Imperial Navy, Admiral Hasegawa had served as Japan's Naval Attache in Washington DC and Chief Delegate to the Naval Conference in 1932. His appointment showed that not only was Formosa under the purview of the Imperial Navy, but as importantly would soon be used as a springboard for active military operations. The key ports were at Takao (Kaoshiung), Keelung, and Makung in the Pescadores. Airfields and supply depots studded the island.

On 8 December 1941 (Far East Time), Japanese war planes took off from Formosa and headed south to target Manila. On this fateful day, the Japanese hit American airfields on Luzon and especially Clark Field. On that same day, Japanese naval transports from Keelung and Takao landed troops in the northern Philippines, an invasion which would only be obscured by the stunning attacks across the Pacific on Pearl Harbor in Hawaii. In a dangerous roll of the geopolitical dice, Imperial Japan had extended the Pacific War to what Tokyo's propagandists liked to say was the *ABCD encirclement*—American, British, Chinese, and Dutch territories. Looking at it another way, Japan had chosen to go to war with half the world. Given its strategic position, Formosa was a nexus of Japan's operations not only for the China coast but also for the Philippines and Southeast Asia.

Indeed, for the first few years of the Pacific War, Formosa was not directly affected, save for the constant mobilizations, rationing, and calls for Japanese patriotism. The island did serve as a logistical hub and production base for Tokyo's expanding war effort. Formosa was also a generally safe area which hosted some notorious Prisoner of War camps (POW) camps for captured allied servicemen.

Allied Prison Camps

Between 1942 and 1945, over 4300 Allied prisoners languished in the Taiwan camps—described as some of the worst in the Far East. Approximately 10 percent of prisoners died in captivity. British, Australian, and Dutch soldiers were scattered among 14 camps, the largest being Taihoku Camp #6 just outside Taipei. On 19 June 1945, 14 captured American airmen were executed at the infamous Taihoku camp. For other POWs, the mix was torture, drudgery, and slave labor; for example, POWs were forced to work at the Kinkaseki copper mine, the largest in the Japanese empire.[37] (Never Forgotten POWTaiwan.org.)

> *POW Camp Kinkaseki* The dark legacy of Taiwan's Japanese POW camps for Allied soldiers is largely unknown or has been forgotten. Between 1942 and 1945, over 4000 Allied servicemen languished in such facilities, described as among the worst detention camps in the Far East. Most of the captives were Australian, British, or Dutch. More than 1100 British and Commonwealth captives were held at the notorious Kinkaseki Camp near the northern port of Keelung. Between December 1942 and March 1945, the inmates were force-marched to a nearby copper mine where they would work in dangerous and grueling conditions. Food was scarce, disease was common, and production quotas were inhumane. Many of the POWs died. Kinkaseki was closed in March 1945 as copper ore production could not be shipped out of Taiwan as Allied navies had taken a toll on Japanese merchant shipping. POWs were transferred to other prison facilities until the war's end. Survivors were evacuated on 6 September 1945 by American and British naval vessels. Between 27 and 42 percent of Allied POWs in the Far East were killed or died in Japanese captivity as compared with 1–2 percent of those held by the Germans or Italians.
> *Source*: Never Forgotten POWTaiwan.org

The war came to Formosa in October 1944 when American bombers began to hit the island in preparation for General Douglas MacArthur's massive amphibious landings in the Philippines. From 12 to 16 October 1944, the US Navy third fleet commenced carrier operations against Japanese airbases on Formosa. In the ensuing battles, large numbers of Japanese aircraft were destroyed, paving the way for the subsequent American landings in Leyte in the Philippines.

In massive air raids in November, Takao, Taihoku, and Keelung ports were hit hard by US airpower.

Formosa's fate in the Pacific War was decided at Pearl Harbor during a late July meeting among President Franklyn D. Roosevelt, General Douglas

MacArthur, and Admiral Chester Nimitz. Originally, US Navy Admiral Chester Nimitz had planned for the invasion of Formosa, "Operation Causeway" as the back door to the Japanese islands. Nimitz would consider bypassing Luzon and going directly for Formosa. General MacArthur, personally committed to liberating the Philippines, pressed for a strategy for striking the Philippines first. Though MacArthur made his case for landings in Luzon later in the year, most of the Navy brass favored hitting Formosa. For months, the Navy plan was a viable option until in reality American ground resources for the Formosan campaign would have to wait until the war in Europe was over. The decision to attack Luzon in December was thus made. Formosa was spared a direct American assault.[38]

There was little the Japanese could do on Formosa except wait for the inevitable. In December 1944, Admiral Hasegawa was replaced by Army General Ando Rikichi, a clear sign that the last-ditch defense of the island would be in the hands of the dogged Imperial Army.

By 1945, even hardline Japanese knew the war was lost; the only question was how and when it would end. In the final months of the conflict, Formosa saw the Allied noose tighten but did not face invasion nor massive population dislocations. A largely intact Japanese garrison and civilian population were marooned in Formosa in the closing weeks of the Pacific War. For the Japanese, both the military and the large civilian community in Taihoku and elsewhere, the end would come soon enough.

Notes

1. Buruma, Ian. *Inventing Japan From Empire to Economic Miracle*, pp. 24–25.
2. Kim, Seung-young. "Russo-Japanese Rivalry Over Korean Buffer at the Beginning of the 20th Century and its Implications," *Diplomacy & Statecraft*, Vol. 16, No. 4, 2005, p. 620.
3. Ibid., p. 621.
4. Paine, S. C. M. *The Sino/Japanese War of 1894–1895*, Cambridge: Cambridge University Press, 2003, p. 4.
5. Ibid., p. 265.
6. Foreign Relations of the United States (FRUS), Vol. 2, 1895, pp. 200–202.
7. Op. cit., Sino-Japanese War, pp. 287–289.
8. Op. cit., p. 3.
9. Op. cit., Inventing Japan, p. 50.

10. Kerr, George. *Formosa Licensed Revolution and the Home Rule Movement 1895–1945*, Honolulu: University of Hawaii Press, 1974, pp. 9–12.
11. Goddard, W. G. *Formosa; A Study in Chinese History*, pp. 129–131.
12. Ibid., pp. 132–136.
13. Taiwan A New History, pp. 174–175.
14. Op. cit., Formosa, pp. 143–145.
15. Op. cit., *Formosa Licensed Revolution*, pp. 21–23.
16. Ibid., pp. 25–28.
17. Formosa Goddard, p. 159.
18. Formosa Licensed Revolution, pp. 75–77.
19. Ibid., pp. 60–61.
20. Ibid., p. 93.
21. *Japan Yearbook*, 1935, p. 1118.
22. Huashan, 1914, Creative Park, Taipei, Taiwan.
23. Op. cit., Yearbook 1935, p. 1116.
24. Ching, Leo, T. S. *Becoming Japanese; Colonial Taiwan and the Politics of Identity Formation*, Berkeley, CA: University of California Press, 2001, p. 15.
25. Ibid., pp. 17–18.
26. Formosa, Goddard, pp. 172–173.
27. *Japan Year book 1935*, Foreign Affairs Association of Japan–Tokyo Kenkyusha Press, 1935, pp. 1096–1097.
28. Ibid., pp. 1098–1099.
29. Taiwan A New History, p. 218, 222–223.
30. Ibid., p. 227.
31. Formosa Licensed Revolution, pp. 151–152.
32. Ibid., pp. 161–168.
33. Ibid., pp. 169–177.
34. Taiwan A New History, pp. 240–243.
35. Formosa Licensed Revolution, p. 196.
36. "The Most Beautiful: The War Films of Shirley Yamaguchi & Setsuko Hara," Japan Society/New York, March 21–April 4, 2015.
37. Never Forgotten POW Taiwan.org
38. Spector, Ronald. *Eagle Against the Sun; The American War with Japan*, New York: Free Press, 1985, pp. 417–419.
Preparations for Formosa's occupation were planned at the Naval School for Military Government and Administration based at Columbia University in New York. Up to two thousand American officers were trained for an operation which was called off in favor of General MacArthur's landings in the Philippines.

CHAPTER 2

Return to Chinese Rule 1945–1950

Plans for Formosa's return to China were codified in the shadow of the pyramids.

Amid the British colonial settings of the Mena House, just outside Cairo, American President Franklin D. Roosevelt, British Prime Minister Winston Churchill, and China's Generalissimo Chiang Kai-shek met in November 1943. The venue for such a high-profile diplomatic conference, among the verdant gardens and palatial architecture, was in itself extraordinary given that just a year earlier, massed German/Italian armies poised to take the Suez Canal were turned back at the pivotal battle of El Alamein. Though the guns were now silent here in Egypt, the war in both the Western and Pacific fronts was not over. Importantly, the outcome against the Axis powers remained far from certain.

The Cairo Conference, as it was known, provided both the American and British leaders a first meeting with China's Chiang Kai-shek. A US State Department history relates:

> At the series of meetings in Cairo, Roosevelt outlined his vision for postwar Asia. He wanted to establish the Republic of China as one of his "Four Policemen." This concept referred to a vision for a cooperative world order in which a dominant power in each major region would be responsible for keeping the peace there. Weak as the Republic of China would inevitably be after the war, it would still be the major power in Asia, and it could help prevent renewed Japanese expansionism and oversee decolonization under a trustee system.

To secure this future, he sought a commitment from Chiang Kai-shek that China would not try to expand across the continent or control decolonizing nations, and in return, he offered a guarantee that the territories stolen from China by Japan—including Manchuria, the island of Taiwan, and the Pescadores Islands—would be returned to Chinese sovereignty.[1]

Under the terms of the Cairo agreement, those territories such as Formosa and the Pescadores which Japan "had stolen" (in itself very strong language for a diplomatic declaration) would be restored to the Republic of China.

The agreement stated in part:

"The Three Great Allies are fighting this war to restrain and punish the aggression of Japan. They covet no gain for themselves and have no thought of territorial expansion.

It is their purpose that Japan shall be stripped of all the islands in the Pacific which she has seized or occupied since the beginning of the first World War in 1914, and that all the territories Japan has stolen from the Chinese, such as Manchuria, Formosa, and the Pescadores, shall be restored to the Republic of China."[2]

In a memorable Fireside chat to Americans at home and serving abroad on Christmas Eve 1943, Franklin D. Roosevelt (FDR) told his radio audience,

"At Cairo, Prime Minister Churchill and I spent four days with the Generalissimo, Chiang Kai-shek. It was the first time that we had (had) an opportunity to go over the complex situation in the Far East with him personally. We were able not only to settle upon definite military strategy, but also to discuss certain long-range principles which we believe can assure peace in the Far East for many generations to come. Those principles are as simple as they are fundamental. They involve the restoration of stolen property to its rightful owners, and the recognition of the rights of millions of people in the Far East to build up their own forms of self-government without molestation."

FDR added, "I met in the Generalissimo a man of great vision, (and) great courage, and a remarkably keen understanding of the problems of today and tomorrow. Today we and the Republic of China are closer together than ever before in deep friendship and in unity of purpose."[3]

Following the Japanese surrender in August 1945, units of the Chinese Nationalist government brought about Taiwan's Retrocession to the central government on 25 October. Yet, in what is often presented as a seamless transfer from the Japanese occupiers to regained Chinese sovereignty is a complicated story in itself.

Large numbers of Japanese civilians and indeed units of the Imperial Army were still on the island. The formal surrender by General Ando again belied the complex process which was necessary both to secure the Japanese surrender and to transfer units of the Chinese Nationalist military to Taiwan. Beyond the physical hurdles, there were the equally challenging psychological barriers which would soon be encountered between the Formosan people and the Chinese mainlanders.

The Nationalist/KMT mantra was that the people on Taiwan should be happy to be rid of the yoke of Japanese colonialism, and correspondingly rejoin their Chinese countrymen. Hesitation by some locals to embrace their liberation by the Republic of China (ROC) government was put down to the fact that Japanese colonial policies had either brainwashed or subverted the character of the local Chinese. This could change with time.

Many Taiwanese, most of whose ethnicity was rooted in coastal Fukien province, nonetheless saw themselves as part of a far more socially advanced and prosperous society with Chinese characteristics but not necessarily under the central government. Though Formosa had been a restive place both for the Qing Dynasty and for the Japanese colonialists, there was also the reality that the island, even before the Japanese seizure in 1895, had a unique character and more advanced socio-economic foundation.

Thus, the simple Nationalist narrative that the Taiwanese were grateful for their liberation from the Japanese, while generally true, soon became mired and blurred in social, economic, and political misunderstandings with the Mainland government.

General Chen Yi, the former Governor of coastal Fukien province, was appointed as Governor General of the Taiwan Provincial Administration as well as the chief of the powerful military Garrison Command. In an early press conference, Governor Chen promised "to act in accordance with the teachings of the Republic's founder (Sun Yat-sen), carry out the Three Principles of the People, liberate our Taiwan brethren from slavery, and then persevere to build a strong, healthy, prosperous Taiwan." In comments to the foreign press in 26 September, the new Governor stressed on the concept that Taiwan was a special case and could not be administered like other provinces. He stated, "After the retrocession of Taiwan to Nationalist China, we will first consider the problem of education. We will rapidly expand the use of kuo-yu (Mandarin), restore the study of Chinese history and education."[4]

Appointing Chen Yi as Governor proved a double-edged sword. Chen had studied in Japan, and also had attended the Japanese Army's military academy, and later married a Japanese woman. Chen's service to Nationalist China and the KMT earned him merit; he played an important role in suppressing warlords through the Northern Expedition and later suppressed a rebellion in Fukien in 1934. He was appointed Governor of Fukien, a post he held until 1944. In a sense, Chen understood the Japanese almost too well and could serve as a bridge to help the social transfer of Taiwan from Imperial Japan's rule to China's regained control. In another sense, Chen Yi was a classic Chinese warlord without the honorific title. The latter would soon prove disastrous.

Yet, the political vacuum after the Japanese formal surrender on 2 September and the arrival of the Nationalists was notable. As Ramon Myers states, "For some weeks after Japan's formal surrender, Japanese officials in Taiwan continued their rule, waiting for someone to arrive to whom they could hand it over. On October 16, an advance party of Nationalist troops disembarked at Keelung, followed the next day with forty small U.S. ships bringing the 70th Division to Keelung." Chen I landed in Taipei, arrived on 24 October, and on the next day in a ceremony at Taipei's Public Auditorium marked Japan's transfer of Taiwan to the national central government.

Japan's last Governor Ando Rikichi signed the surrender document. By 30 October, orders were issued to all Japanese troops to surrender their weapons. Chinese troops subsequently interred the Japanese; yet given their large numbers and poor available transport, by February 1946, there were still 322,000 Japanese in detention.[5]

After the collapse of Japanese rule, the island of Taiwan suffered serious shortages in both security personnel and civilian government workers. As Myers reminds us, in 1945, Japan's colonial bureaucracy had a staff of 84,559 people. The police force stood at just under 13,000 and the military garrison was 195,000.

The ROC government could send only 28,000 to run and police Taiwan. By August 1946, the police numbered 9337 but soon declined to 8378. Military forces were stretched too—the initial divisions sent from the Mainland in 1945 to accept the surrender were soon posted back to the Mainland to stem the communist tide in the worsening civil war. Fewer than 5000 troops remained in autumn 1946. Thus, the combined police–military presence on the island was near 13,000, just over 6 percent of the Japanese presence.

Equally, the bureaucracy was decimated. The Japanese administration included 84,559 people, of which 47,000 were Taiwanese. Myers relates that under the ROC, the bureaucracy stood at 44,451 and included only 9951 islanders. In other words, some 36,000 Taiwanese had lost their jobs.[6]

So here we see a curious paradox. In the wake of the war's end and privations, Taiwan is returned to China but in effect had far less security than previously and, more importantly, has now alienated an educated and competent sector of the population. Resentment among the civil service, a respected rung in the social ladder, going back to Mandarin times, was allowed to fester.

In the meantime after Taiwan retrocession, the civil war was raging on the Mainland between Mao's communists backed by the Soviets, and the Nationalist government with now wavering American support.

Economically, Japanese Formosa has been a relatively prosperous place with a working transport, industrial, and agricultural sector. Wartime air raids and the destruction of port facilities played a role in the overall disruption. For example, in 1945, the total number of railway cars hauled amounted to only 25 percent of those hauled in 1944. By the end of 1946, only 80 percent of the railway system had been restored. Given Formosa's colonial dependence on Japanese markets and supplies, such as fertilizer, skewed the entire economy. The curse of runaway inflation soon followed. Between 1944 and 1945, prices jumped over 530 percent. Rice, a staple of the local diet, saw prices surge throughout 1946 and 1947.[7]

Under Chen Yi's tenure, there was a new Monopoly Bureau which controlled the production of camphor, matches, liquor, and tobacco. Besides controlling many of the former Japanese industries and agricultural enterprises, the government set up a bureau to regulate trade. Widespread economic controls were put in place which discouraged enterprise and in turn encouraged cronyism and corruption in the post-war economy.

As Ramon Myers stresses in the landmark book, *A Tragic Beginning*, "Statism generated additional problems that aggravated the economic crisis created by the war. As state regulation inhibited production and commerce, inflation increased, and living standards declined." Black markets thrived and as Myers adds of Chen Yi's approach, "On the whole, his statist, interventionist economic policy exacerbated rather than alleviated Taiwan's economic crisis—a crisis that heightened tensions between Mainlanders and Taiwanese."[8]

American policy toward China was beginning to witness a political sea change.

Recall that during the Pacific War, Nationalist China was one of the Big 5 Allies (Britain, China, France, USSR, and the USA). Moreover, China was one of the signatory founders of the UN, the multinational organization which came into being in October 1945, ironically at the very same time as Taiwan retrocession to the ROC. Still with Mao's communists expanding their influence, especially in formerly Japanese controlled Manchuria, Washington was pressing for a political compromise, among China's political factions.

A State Department policy paper written in the waning weeks of the Pacific War conceded: "The Chinese Communists will probably be exercising control over substantial areas of northern, northeastern, central and eastern China … on relaxation of Japanese control the Chinese Communists will occupy Manchuria." The report clearly warns, "Failure of the Kuomintang and the Chinese Communists to unite will in all probability lead to the formal establishment of two distinct political and military entities in China, with the Kuomintang controlling one and the Communists the other. The result of this division of China into two separate spheres of power is likely to be internal strife."[9]

In December 1945, President Harry Truman, in a message to General George Marshall, stated, "It is the firm belief of this Government that a strong, united, and democratic China is of the utmost importance to the success of this United Nations organization and for world peace. A China disorganized and divided, either by foreign aggression, such as that undertaken by the Japanese, or by violent internal strife, is an undermining influence to world stability and peace." Truman added, "The Government of the U.S. believes it essential: That a cessation of hostilities be arranged between the armies of the National Government and the Chinese communists." He added forcefully, "The U.S. and other United Nations have recognized the present National Government of the Republic of China as the only legal government in China. It is the proper instrument to achieve the objective of a unified China."[10]

In the midst of the political maelstrom on Mainland China, Formosa was already feeling the ill winds. The island was awash with rumors and a raft of conspiracy theories which rapidly spread through society and found receptive listeners in the street markets. One rumor was that China had sold Taiwan to the USA in return for military credits to pursue the civil war. Others spoke of large numbers of American troops coming to the island to create a string of military bases. Some spoke about the return of the Japanese.

American Consul Ralph Blake, in a blunt assessment report, warned, "Public uneasiness reflects the uncertainties of political and economic conditions both on the mainland and on Taiwan. The seeming imminence of a large civil war on the mainland is felt here. The continuing influx to Taiwan of people of all classes from all coastal areas (with a rising percentage from the poorest levels) brings conflicting interpretations of conditions across the channel."[11]

February 28, The Tragedy

The tragic 28 February 1947 incident was sparked over the selling of allegedly contraband cigarettes. Officers from the Monopoly Bureau questioned, then assaulted, a 40-year-old widow selling cigarettes in Taipei. The incident soon turned into a confrontation between the officials and a group of angry onlookers. A bystander was shot and killed and before long a mob converged on the Taipei Police Bureau. Violence spread like wildfire throughout Taipei and Keelung, with attacks on Mainlanders and government property. Martial law was imposed.

Between 28 February and the next week, widespread disorder spread throughout many of the island's towns and local committees demand the ouster of the unpopular Governor Chen Yi. Correspondingly, the authorities had few security resources in Taiwan at the time of the uprising. For example, the Japanese stationed about 200,000 troops and police on the island in the 1940s; after retrocession to the Nationalists, there were only about 10,000 police island-wide.

As violence widened against anything perceived as Chinese, mobs attack, beat, and often murder Mainlanders and burn their businesses. Slogans like "Abolish the Monopoly Bureau" and "Down with Chen Yi's Commercial Trading Company" soon radicalized to "Let Taiwan Rule Itself." Revolutionary political demands were not tempered by repeated calls and broadcasts by the Governor General for calm and conciliation. Chen was hesitant to ask the central government for urgent assistance, as this would represent a "loss of face" for the Governor's status and an admission that matters had spiraled out of control, as they already had.

Indeed, the ROC government's tardy response must be seen in the light of its increasingly embattled position on the Mainland where effective combat troops, to oppose the widening civil war with the communists, were sorely needed.

On 8 and 9 March, military reinforcements from the Mainland landed in Keelung and Kaohsiung and the impending counterattack commenced.

American reactions to the 28 February incident and the widening disorders were nervous and but couched in the opinion that the USA could still remedy the problem.

A 3 March memo sent to the US Embassy in Nanking stated:

> "After gravest consideration Consulate concludes only practicable solution would be immediate American intervention in its own right or on behalf of UN. ... American prestige high and intervention profoundly desired by Formosans. ... Formosans assume UN control would be predominantly American. They frequently express desire for democratic political training and desire ultimate government of Formosa by Formosans representing the island in the Central Government."

The Consular report, nonetheless, warned, "Civil war on Formosa is the most probable alternative."[12]

KMT General Pai Chung-hsi, who visited Taiwan, stressed that "Formosan-Chinese have been misled by long Japanese indoctrination which taught them to vilify the Chinese government, the people and the troops Japanese educational influence will be eradicated." He added that "Formosans should have a larger share in government. The administrative structure will become that of a regular province ... public lands (which occupy 70 percent of the island's area) will be opened to private agricultural use."[13]

Despite the growing disorders, the besieged central government in Nanking hesitated to send scarce troops to Taiwan which were desperately needed on the Mainland. Chiang Kai-shek ordered his local Governor not to take revenge. "I ask that you strongly restrain your forces, preventing them from taking revenge." Yet, despite orders, the unruly situation produced a terrible backlash. General Peng Meng-chi, Kaohsiung commander, wanted to "teach the insurgents a lesson" and massacres followed in both Kaohsiung and Tainan. Despite Peng's government-initiated violence, much of the killing was against the direct orders of the Generalissimo and Chen I.[14]

There were a plethora of problems which beset Taiwan after its return from Japanese rule. First and foremost was the KMT government's view that the islanders should rejoice at being liberated from Japan and thus embrace the Chinese motherland. Many Taiwanese, who were not particularly fond of Japan, nonetheless knew that their island was a far more prosperous and socially advanced place than many of the Mainland provinces. The central government viewed Taiwan as a source of resources and not as an equal player among other provinces. Ineffective and corrupt economic mismanagement also bedeviled the transfer. Equally, the government maintained too few troops and police on the island, allowing initial disorders to boil over and spread.

According to Dr. Myers, "Bureaucratic corruption and troop misbehavior were other problems for which the KMT was to some extent responsible. More important, it was responsible for the basic problem; the obtuse, incompetent leadership of Chen Yi ... there is some truth to General Wedemeyer's report made in August 1947 to the U.S. Secretary of State; 'Chen I and his henchmen ruthlessly, corruptly and avariciously imposed their regime upon a happy and amenable population.'"[15]

Estimates vary wildly on the number of both during the rebellion and the subsequent military and police crackdowns throughout Taiwan. The numbers of people killed by the Nationalist forces ranged from 1000 to 100,000. According to *A Tragic Beginning*, strong evidence that "the number of Taiwanese and Mainlanders killed was around 8,000 at most."[16]

"White Terror" on Formosa The tragedy of the 28 February 1947 uprising did not end in the tumultuous weeks following the bloody civil disturbances across the island. After the still-jolted Taiwan Provincial Government declared Martial Law on 19 May 1949, a period of what came to be called the "White Terror" would shadow Formosa.

In its quest to root out "subversives," the new KMT rulers cracked down on a wide spectrum of dissidents ranging from communists, to Taiwanese and aboriginal intellectuals, and anybody with a political streak not conforming to the new Chinese nationalist order. Disappearances and detentions became common. The worst excesses came in the three years following the 28 February incident.

According to former Democratic Progressive Party (DPP) legislator Hsieh Tsung-min, "there were about 29,000 cases of political persecution during the Martial Law era, including 140,000 people. An estimated 3000–4000 people were executed."

"In those days many people perished," stated Prof. Lee Shiao-feng of Taipei's Shih Hsin University. Prof. Lee stated that cases during the White Terror fell into several categories: arrest communists or left wing partisans, crush the Taiwanese independence movement,

> and purge the Aboriginal elites. Of the political cases between 1949 and 1960, approximately 2000 people were executed and 8000 were sentenced to severe punishment.
> The White Terror, according to "A Tragic Beginning," must be nonetheless viewed in the context of the times; the ousting of Japanese rule from Taiwan was followed by what the new KMT rulers assumed would be a grateful pro-Chinese populace.
> This, combined with the clumsy mishandling of a sensitive social order by the corrupt new Governor Chen I, was a recipe for conflict. Moreover, the ongoing civil war on the Mainland, coinciding with the 28 February incident, and lasting and intensifying for next few years, would be conducive to crackdowns on dissent in the newly freed Province of Taiwan. Then there was the Cold War itself.
> Martial law was lifted on 15 July 1987 during Chiang Ching-kuo's presidency.
> *Source*: "White Terror Exhibit Unveils Part of the Truth," *Taipei Times* 20 May 2005. P. 2. <u>A Tragic Beginning: The Taiwan Uprising of February 28, 1947.</u> Lai Tse-Han, Ramon H. Myers and Wei Wou (Stanford, CA: Stanford University Press, 1991), pp. 177–180.

George Kerr served as American Vice Counsel in Taipei. Having visited Formosa during the Japanese period and being fully aware of the possibilities for the island in the post-war period, Kerr offered an invaluable and penetrating overview of Taiwan in the wake of the 28 February uprising.

In his famous April 1947 Memorandum for the Ambassador on the Situation in Taiwan, Kerr advises somewhat surprisingly:

> "However bitter their criticism of local administrative policy before these uprisings, there can be no question that the Formosan-Chinese have felt loyalty to the Central Government and towards the Generalissimo. Fifty years under Japanese rule had sharpened their sense of Chinese nationality and race and in doing so developed a strong sense of island-wide social unity. Formosans have been ambitious to see Taiwan become a model province of China."

He added that "It may therefore be said with a high degree of assurance that as of March 1, 1947, communism in any form was of most negligible importance on Taiwan." He warned, however, "a local form of communism is not only possible but believed to be a highly probable development if economic organization collapses under the pressure of continued military occupation." Kerr advised that if the national government did not allow for more local rule, institutions, and a revived economy, the island would have to be controlled by a costly and unpopular military occupation. He warned, "A state of near anarchy is a distinct possibility for Formosa by the end of 1947 if drastic efforts to revise policy and effect government reforms (free of military pressure) are not undertaken speedily."[17]

Kerr surmised, "Taiwan was returned to China as an outstanding economic asset, an example of the advanced technological economy towards which all other provinces of China are striving ... economic stability and expansion must be founded on a sound political and social administration. Now is the time to act."[18]

A sullen calm permeated Taiwan in the spring of 1947. Not even two years since the Japanese had departed, the island was torn by political divisions caused largely by the heavy-handed administration of Governor Chen Yi. At least 50,000 government troops were now garrisoned on the island to tamp down further violence.

Obviously political changes were painfully overdue. The appointment of Dr. Wei Tao-ming by the Nanking government was such a move intended both to change the narrative on the disgraced Chen Yi and to really try to make a potentially prosperous province reach its potential. Yet, one must recall that quick and seamless political solutions were not easily achieved in the midst of the growing civil war on the Mainland. Chiang Kai-shek had only moved the capital back to Nanking in May 1946, and the pure bureaucratic and political housekeeping chores of the new post-war government were still in flux.

The KMT's first uneasy years on the island, such as the violent and brutal 28 February incident, against the backdrop of both Mao's looming military threat from the Mainland and the Truman administration's tepid political/military support for Formosa set the stage for miscalculations, bureaucratic misfeasance, and malfeasance.

American Ambassador to China John Leighton Stuart advised the Secretary of State, "the fairly complete change of government structure in Taiwan as a direct consequence of the rebellion there may now be considered as an official admission of the failure of the previous regime." Again, despite Formosa's formidable economic infrastructure and potential, there was the undertow of state "monopoly" enterprises which not only constricted free commerce but equally allowed for wider patronage and corruption.

George Kerr was becoming increasingly frustrated in Taipei. In a May memo to Washington, he warned bluntly: "Under present Chinese policy it is believed probable that Formosa will succumb to communism in the near future." He cited the "recent massacres, military subjugation (an estimated 50,000 troops now there) and superficial gestures in answer to popular reform demands have estranged Formosans from the mainland." Even the more reserved Ambassador Stuart opined, "Secret police activities increasing ... impression spreading the new civilian government powerless to control military or is giving it free hand."[19]

As the year progressed, by November, the situation failed to improve again prompting Ambassador Stuart to admit, "news from Formosa continues to indicate maladministration, smoldering discontent and organization of revolutionary activities under capable leadership with objective of virtual autonomy." Significantly, Stuart stated that, "Gimo was aware of the situation and expressed hearty endorsement in principle of some form of joint Chinese-American administration of Formosa for a limited period of years with the emphasis on economic reconstruction."[20]

Gathering Storm in China

By 1948, the rapidly widening civil war on the Mainland dominated the headlines. The discussion concerning Taiwan was now largely being viewed as a possible safe haven or even last-ditch redoubt for the Nationalist government. American policymakers were increasingly nervous not only about an impending defeat of the allied Chinese government to the communists, but equally unsure about how the long-forgotten island of Formosa would fit into the new political puzzle.

Ambassador John Leighton Stuart, from his vantage point in Nanking, watched the drama unfold. Stuart, born to American missionary parents in China, was fluent in both the language (dialect) and the customs. In late December in a cable to the Secretary of State, he admitted candidly, if diplomatically, "It must be admitted, however, that Chinese activities in Taiwan since the liberation from Japs, have tended to dissipate enthusiasm with which Taiwanese anticipated return to Chinese sovereignty."

The Ambassador added,

> "In present national crisis CAF (Chinese Air Force) and Navy are already in process of transferring their major installations to Taiwan. Large numbers of well-to-do Chinese have already established themselves on the island ...

it is possible that other sections Chinese Government itself will evacuate to island ... downfall National Government might be signal for even wider spread insurrection. We assume, however, that Chinese possess necessary force on island to suppress any such activities."

He added that while the Chinese Air Force was asking the United States to assist in transferring heavy equipment from Shanghai to Taiwan and other such transport activities, "This raises the problem of degree we are prepared to go in assisting Chinese movement to Taiwan."

Significantly, Ambassador Stuart warned, "We feel that in view of delicate relationship between Taiwanese and Chinese Nationalist Government, US Government should avoid, through action of any of its agencies in China, giving appearance of assisting transfer of authority of Nationalist Government to Taiwan."[21]

In the bigger picture, events on the Mainland were spiraling out of control. Hyperinflation was as big a menace to the Nationalists as the encroaching communist forces. In fact, the dilution of the money supply and the loss of all faith in the currency played a large role in the popular discontent and corruption in the final years of Chiang's rule. In August 1948, prices, as measured by the Shanghai wholesale price index, were more than three million times those of the pre-war half year January to June 1937. "In the first 7 months of 1948 prices increased more than 45 times and the black market rate for the United States dollar notes increased over 50 times," cites a report on US economic aid. The report added, "In the mid-summer of 1948 there was a sharp increase in the velocity of currency circulation which sent prices to astronomical figures." "Bushel baskets were required for currency transactions. The currency had become almost worthless as a medium of exchange."[22]

Hyperinflation, loss of faith in the government, and the military onslaught of Mao's communists were among the dark clouds on the Nationalist horizons. In August 1948, the introduction of a new gold Yuan currency to back the old currency at a rate of 1 gold Yuan to 3 million Chinese National Yuan failed to stop the free fall.

By the following spring, the gold Yuan was worthless and quoted between 5 million and 10 million to $1 US! dollar! Foreign aid for the Chinese government since VJ Day (1945) amounted to approximately $2.25 billion, of which the USA had provided 90 percent in the form of grants and loans. Aid was divided equally between military and economic assistance. In fact, Washington's support to Nanking amounted to more than 50 percent of the Nationalist government, a sum larger than US assistance to any Western European country.[23]

During the autumn of 1948, the military situation became bleak. Manchuria and North China were lost. In mid-January, Tientsin fell and Peiping surrendered in late January.

In the early days of January 1949, the National Security Council instructed staff to formulate a Taiwan policy statement. The initial draft NSC 34/1 listed four policy alternatives (a) occupying Taiwan with US forces, (b) negotiating "base rights" on Taiwan (the Pentagon's approach), (c) backing the Nationalist government (the China's bloc's approach), and (d) supporting "continued local non-Communist Chinese control" and using our influence wherever possible to discourage the use of Formosa as a refuge for National Government remnants (Central Intelligence Agency (CIA) approach). The Department of State and Defense settled on the fourth option. The new Secretary of State Dean Acheson favored a more nuanced approach which in effect would separate Taiwan from both warring parties on the China Mainland.[24]

Truman Doctrine The Truman Doctrine arose from an address delivered by President Harry Truman before a joint session of Congress on 12 March 1947. According to the State Department, "The immediate cause for the speech was a recent announcement by the British Government that, as of March 31, it would no longer provide military and economic assistance to the Greek Government in its civil war against the Greek Communist Party. Truman asked Congress to support the Greek Government against the Communists."

Truman argued that the USA could no longer stand by and allow the forcible expansion of Soviet totalitarianism into free, independent nations, because American national security now depended upon more than just the physical security of American territory. Importantly then in a "break with its traditional avoidance of extensive foreign commitments beyond the Western Hemisphere during peacetime," the Truman Doctrine committed the USA to actively offering assistance to preserve the political integrity of democratic nations when such an offer was deemed to be in the best interest of the USA.

> Yet, during this same momentous period in the Far East, events were quickly unraveling both in China and soon in Korea. While the Truman Administrations' relationship with the ROC, now in exile on Taiwan, were clouded by very understandable American frustrations with the Chinese Nationalists during the civil war of 1945–1949, up to the point where weeks before the Korean conflict, the USA was plotting an overthrow of Chiang Kai-shek. Yet, the Truman Administration was not watching unfolding events on the divided Korean peninsula either. When war broke out on 25 June 1950, Harry Truman, to his credit, did an abrupt about face and sent troops and aid to Korea and before long Taiwan. The Truman Doctrine now applied to East Asia too.
>
> *Source*: US Department of State Office of the Historian history. state.gov

Since mid-October, the CIA had predicted that barring US intervention, Taiwan "would succumb to the Chinese Communists by the end of 1950." Talk of UN Trusteeship was in the air. The State Department was shuffling political options and alternatives, few of which included Chiang's KMT setting up on the island.

The Deputy Assistant Secretary for Far Eastern Affairs stated bluntly in February 1950, that "the United States occupy Taiwan, conduct a plebiscite, and create a new nation on the island." By May, the State Department's Dean Rusk would propose an American sponsored *coup d'état* on Taiwan, and led Dean Acheson to believe that he had no other viable alternative. Sun Li-jen, a Nationalist General of standing, would be the American point man for the operation.[25]

After the Nationalist government's forced retreat to Formosa in 1949 and the first few perilous months in the shadow of Mao's communists, American diplomacy focused on economic support to stabilize the island but showed little political appetite to extend military assistance in the wake of Chiang Kai-shek's losing of the civil war. Interestingly, Taiwan was viewed from an American context as being vital to the food supply and defense of Japan, rather than in the context of a regained province of a China in tatters from civil war.

On 31 May, less than a month before the outbreak of hostilities on the Korean peninsula, a Top Secret State Department Memorandum by Assistant Secretary of State for Far Eastern Affairs, Dean Rusk, outlined an explosive set of options for Taiwan. There was a plan to package three points: Formosa, Recognition of Communist China, and seating to Peking delegation in the UN. Rusk informed Acheson:

> "The Gimo would be approached, probably by Dulles ... with word that (a) the Fall of Formosa was probably Inevitable, (b) the U.S. would do nothing to assist Gimo in preventing this, (c) the only course open to the Gimo to prevent bloodshed was to request UN trusteeship. The U.S. would be prepared to back such a move for trusteeship and would ready the fleet to prevent any armed attack on Formosa while the move for trusteeship was pending."[26]

Clearly, the US government had crossed the political *Rubicon* on China policy; in the wake of the fall of the Mainland to Mao's communists, the Truman Administration was trying to cut its ties with a Nationalist government and prepare Formosa for a future yet to be determined. Events in Korea on 25 June would drastically change the calculations and would ironically save Chiang's embattled Nationalists from a near certain fate.

A few months into the Korean War, the State Department was still toying with the idea of trusteeship for Taiwan. Dean Acheson hoped bringing the Taiwan case before the UN would politically shelter the island from what was an expected Chinese communist seaborne assault. Washington asked the UN General Assembly to include the agenda item "Question of Formosa," which would present and review options for the island's future.

President Truman has stated that the "future status of Formosa must await the restoration of security in the Pacific, a peace settlement with Japan, or consideration by the United Nations." The US move infuriated a curious combination of critics including the USSR as well as Nationalist China. China's representative stated that it was "unprecedented in the United Nations for the Government of one member state to question the right of another State to its territorial possessions. In doing so, the United Stated delegation had taken a very grave step." Taipei's delegate then put forth a line which would be followed for over a decade, "As long as Formosa stood, the communist conquest of the mainland of China could not be completed or consolidated. The island was therefore the bastion of freedom in the whole Far East." Before long, Washington made a political *volte face* and deferred the proposal.²⁷

Thus, 1950 became a pivotal year for Taiwan and the Far East in general. Despite the heralded Truman Doctrine, the USA was about to cut Formosa loose. Clearly, by the early part of 1950, the Truman Administration was determined not to involve itself in what looked like Formosa's last-ditch defense. The Korean War changed the political equation and correspondingly dramatically changed Taiwan's fortunes.

Notes

1. U.S. State Dept./Archive Cairo Conference.
2. U.S. Department of State, In Quest of Peace and Security: Selected Documents on American Foreign Policy, 1941–1951, Washington, DC: GPO, 1951, p. 10.
3. Miller Center/University of Virginia Fireside chat #27 24 December 1943.
4. A Tragic Beginning, Myers, pp. 57–59.
5. Ibid. pp. 62–63.
6. Ibid. p. 65.
7. Ibid. pp. 81–82.
8. Ibid. pp. 87–89.
9. Foreign Relations of the U.S. (FRUS) 1945/Vol. VI/Far East/Japan, p. 564.
10. FRUS 1945, Vol. VII Far East/China, pp. 770–771.
11. FRUS 1947, Vol. VII, Far East/China, pp. 424–425.
12. FRUS 1947, Vol. VII, pp. 433–434.
13. Ibid. p. 446.
14. Op. cit., Tragic Beginning, pp. 149, 155–164.
15. Ibid. pp. 168–171.
16. Ibid. pp. 155, 178.
17. Op. cit. FRUS 1947, Vol. VII, pp. 451–453.
18. Ibid. p. 454.
19. Ibid. pp. 459, 466–468.
20. Ibid. p. 470.
21. FRUS 1948, Vol. VII, pp. 661–662.
22. *United States Relations with China*; With special Reference to the Period 1944–1949. Washington, DC, Department of State, 1949. Pp. 399–400.

Also known as the "White Paper" the State Department book of 1054 pages was published just two months before Mao proclaimed the People's Republic. The exhaustive volume served as an *apologia* for American policy in face of growing criticism of "Who lost China?"
23. Ibid. pp. 400–405.
24. McGlothlen, Ronald. *Controlling the Waves; Dean Acheson and U.S. Foreign Policy in Asia.* New York: Norton, 1993, pp. 91–92.
25. Ibid. pp. 113, 125.
26. USDS Memorandum (Top Secret) 31 May 1950.
27. *Yearbook of the United Nations, 1950.* New York: Department of Public Information, 1951. Pp. 297–298.

CHAPTER 3

Free China; Cold War Fortress 1951–1971

The outbreak of the Korean War in June 1950 made Formosa a vital geopolitical piece on the East Asian game-board and correspondingly gave the Chinese Nationalists a reprieve from a political near-death experience. With an unexpected conflict raging on the Korean peninsula, and in dangerous proximity to Japan, the USA was jolted out of strategic slumber and immediately sought to revive defense ties among regional states. Despite strained relations with the KMT government on Formosa, the Truman White House performed a political *volte face* and took immediate steps to protect Taiwan but, more importantly, integrate the island into a wider defensive cordon not only to assist in the war effort in Korea, but to what would emerge as a wider containment policy of the Chinese mainland.

Just ten days before the onset of hostilities in Korea, General Douglas MacArthur in a *top secret* report warned that Formosa must not be allowed to fall into "the hands of a power unfriendly to the United States" as it "constitutes an enemy salient in the very center of that portion of our position now keyed to Japan, Okinawa and the Philippines." He added that the island "in the hands of the communists can be compared to an unsinkable aircraft carrier" which would threaten American interests. Rephrasing the challenge, MacArthur later viewed Formosa with his well-remembered quip that the unsinkable aircraft carrier can serve as a needed military base, regional food exporter, and political model. "There can be no doubt but that the eventual fate of Formosa largely rests with the United States."[1]

© The Editor(s) (if applicable) and The Author(s) 2017
J.J. Metzler, *Taiwan's Transformation*,
DOI 10.1057/978-1-137-56442-9_3

Korean Interlude

Significantly, by the start of the Korean War in June 1950, the political tables had surprisingly turned to Taiwan's advantage. President Harry Truman ordered the Seventh Fleet into the Formosa Straits "to prevent any attack on Formosa ... as a corollary of this action, I am calling upon the Chinese government on Formosa to cease all air and sea operations against the Mainland. The determination of the future status of Formosa must await the restoration of security in the Pacific, a peace settlement with Japan, or consideration by the United Nations."[2]

Despite quick and decisive UN actions to halt the North Korean aggression and to assemble and deploy a multinational force onto the divided peninsula to stabilize the situation, the summer of 1950 saw serious setbacks for the Seoul government and South Korea. Korean and the bedraggled UN forces were pushed southward to the port of Pusan and what became known as the Pusan Perimeter. What appeared to be a last-ditch stance by the allied forces about to be pushed off the peninsula evoked Dunkirk a decade earlier.[3]

Yet, General Mac Arthur was able to pluck victory from the jaws of imminent defeat. The spectacular amphibious landing in Inchon, which severed the North Korean lines of communications and soon saw South Korean and UN forces on the offensive, was able to nearly turn the tide just three months into the conflict. Starting from the Inchon landings on 15 September and the subsequent recapture of Seoul, the North Korean forces were significantly outflanked and soon routed.

"Continuing operations will take full advantage of our initiative and unified strength to provide for the complete destruction of the enemy and his complete capitulation," assured MacArthur. At the time of the offensive, the UN Command comprised naval forces from eight nations: ground forces from five, and air forces from two. South Korea was largely liberated, and the forces had pursued targets into the North.[4]

In a Security Council Report dated 5 November, General Mac Arthur stated warily, "The United Nations forces in Korea are continuing their drive to the north ... however, presently in certain areas of Korea, the United Nations forces are meting a new foe. ... Chinese communist military units deployed for action against the forces of the United Nations."[5]

In parallel to the fast-unfolding military situation on the Korean peninsula, including the introduction of Chinese communist forces into the fray, the island of Taiwan was by no means safe from attack. In October, a Top

Secret CIA memo conceded, the "communists are now capable of launching an invasion against Formosa with about 200,000 troops and moderate air cover. Although the Chinese Nationalist forces are sufficient in number and material to defend Formosa, lack of staying power, poor command structure, lack of inter-service coordination, questionable morale and shortages of some types of ammunition make their defense capabilities questionable." Yet, the memo concluded that without direct Soviet participation given powerful US naval and air assistance, the Nationalists could hold Formosa.

The memo opined that barring a Soviet decision to participate in a war, an invasion will not be attempted "during the remainder of 1950." The memo added cryptically, however, "in view of current UN interest in Formosa, the Chinese communists have some reason to hope for a favorable political solution."[6]

Indeed, US policy while focused on Korea, wanted to keep the Formosa issue separate from "Any General Assembly move to link the Formosa question to the settlement of the Korean problem and any move to call a conference on Far Eastern problems (including Formosa), prior to a settlement of the Korean problem."[7]

Stabilizing Taiwan's domestic economic situation was no less a challenge. Combined with the defensive shield of the US Navy Seventh Fleet in the Formosa Straits, American economic aid would flow to the island with the intention to "advise" but not "give economic direction" to the Chinese. A statement by Dean Rusk, Assistant Secretary of State for Far Eastern Affairs, stated clearly: "The political purpose of the economic program should be to create on the Island of Formosa a society which has prospect for enduring as a balanced and productive economic system ... the economic objective should not be to erect a structure primarily designed to provide Mainland elements with a short term springboard for realization of their future ambitions."[8]

This statement clearly alluded to Washington's desire to help Taiwan economically, but not to support the KMT government's wider wish and still serious aspiration to return to the Mainland and in turn probably pull the USA back into a renewed civil conflict.

LAND REFORM AND AID FROM A FOREIGN FRIEND

"The large amount of economic aid given to Taiwan by the United States from 1951 to 1965 helped stabilize the currency of the Republic of China, provided the much needed capital for investment and led to the technical know-how from the United States," advised Prof. Yung Wei. The aid was focused not only on infrastructure but also on bringing foreign exchange to cover imports. Yung Wei added that "in an indirect way, the United States economic aid also contributed to the political stability on the island," by restoring credibility of the government.[9]

The period between 1950 and 1958 represented a time of reconstruction and development for Taiwan, which witnessed the transformation of the island from a rural economy into a more industrialized economy according to Prof. Yung Wei.

The ROC government was clearly focused on effective and equitable land reform in Taiwan. Having been jarred and nearly toppled by not having properly addressed land tenure issues among the farmers on Mainland China, the Nationalists, now in exile on Taiwan, made a bold and politically decisive move which would not only reinvigorate the island's agricultural production but equally share and spread land ownership to the tenant farmers. The *Land to the Tiller* program became a signature policy of the ROC's early socio/economic development on Taiwan.

Initial efforts at land reform started in January 1949 with rent reduction on property being the first step. The second stage involved the sale of government land acquired from the Japanese colonial rulers; in this case, large agricultural tracts and land which had been held by Japanese colonizers. Much was rich farmland, which became public property under the newly established ROC government. By June 1951, approximately 100,000 chia (one chia being approximately one hectare), were made available for distribution, the land going to tenant cultivators.[10]

Land reform became a hallmark of Taiwan's socio-economic rebirth. Land reform consisted of three phases: (a) reduction of farm rents; (b) sale of public farmlands; (c) implementation of the *Land to the Tiller* program. "The Land to the Tiller Act" was promulgated in January 1953. That year the government purchased 140,000 hectares of land or 55 percent of all privately tenanted land and then resold it to 195,000 farm families. Significantly, farm tenancy was reduced from 39 percent to 14 percent. At the same time, farm ownership increased from 61 percent to 86 percent. Both purchase and resale prices for land were fixed at 2.3 times the main annual crop yield. Landowners were paid a lump sum, which was 70 percent in commodity bonds and 30 percent in the stocks of three major government enterprises.[11]

> *Neil Jacoby—Mr. "Foreign Aid"* The role of American economic assistance to Taiwan's development is widely admired and recognized as a success story. Yet, one of the key figures in this "foreign aid" program has been largely forgotten. Canadian-born and University of Chicago Economics Ph.D., Neil H. Jacoby was best known as a Dean and Professor at the University of California Graduate School of Business Administration. During the Eisenhower Administration, Dr. Jacoby, since a naturalized American citizen, served on the President's Council of Economic Advisors. Working as a Consultant to the US Agency for International Development (USAID), Jacoby chronicled the compelling story of American economic assistance which led to Taiwan's development. Between 1951 and 1965, the USA delivered $1.4 billion in "foreign aid" to Taiwan which Dr. Jacoby analyses in his *"An Evaluation of U.S. Economic Aid to Free China."*
>
> Source: Dwight D. Eisenhower Presidential Library/Eisenhower.archives.gov

In parallel to the *Land to the Tiller* program was an extensive American economic aid program which would help the island achieve self-sustaining economic growth. Operating through the Agency for International Development (AID) in the crucial period 1951–1965, the US program focused $1.4 billion in assistance to Taiwan.

A crucial if now forgotten study *"An Evaluation of U.S. Economic Aid to Free China 1951–1965,"* written by Prof. Neil Jacoby, a University of Chicago Ph.D., offered an extensive overview of the success story.

The program found an island which was receptive to help. "A legacy of Japanese colonial period was a strategic determinant of the rapid pace of Taiwan's development after 1951," writes report author Neil Jacoby. The islanders "human attitudes, skills, and institutions" were favorable to development, and thus helped reconstruction. "During 1951–1965, Taiwan's economy maintained a higher growth rate than any other in Asia except Japan," the author added. The numbers were amazing: real Gross National Product (GNP) stood at 7.6 percent and GNP rose from $879 million in 1951 to $2.4 billion in 1965, an increase of 173 percent. There was also a corresponding shift from agriculture to industry.[12]

The structural shifts were significant in which the public sector was declining in favor of a rising private sector. Though farms were privately owned, overall private enterprises rose from 45 percent to 62 percent during the 1951–1963 period. Government-owned firms fell from 55 percent to 38 percent in this period. During this period, Prof. Jacoby cites an "enormous increase in the private enterprise population of Taiwan and a vigorous growth of the private sector" from 68,000 to 227,000 firms. Businesses grew from 1000 to 11,000 in this same period.[13]

Overall, Taiwan society was becoming more healthy with the eradication of tropical diseases, such as Malaria, and more literate, with a literacy rate jumping from 57 percent to 76 percent between 1951 and 1963. The ROC government's focus on compulsory, universal, and free public schools underlined this achievement.[14]

The two major thrusts of AID development were to elevate development as a national goal and to foster private enterprise. Initially, when the ROC regained Taiwan from the Japanese, the island was saddled with many large-scale government-owned firms. Equally, many of the Chinese government bureaucrats who had come to Taiwan did not favor wide-scale privatizations. Yet, again, the concept of "lessons learned" from the Mainland debacle gave a genuine impetus to the ROC in its new incarnation on Taiwan.

Given that government officials were initially not too well disposed to a classic free market model, "AID emphasis on private enterprise came during the latter part of the aid period after the environment and Chinese attitudes were favorable," Jacoby asserts.[15]

"Supercharged by $1.5 billion of external aid over 1951–1965, Taiwan's economy was propelled from deep dependence into a state of self-sustaining development within a span of fifteen years," the report stated, adding, "When Taiwan is compared with Korea, Philippines, Thailand and Turkey ... it is found that not only was the annual growth rate of Taiwan's GNP much higher, but that increase in GNP per dollar of aid was higher." It added the 7.6 percent annual growth of Taiwan's GNP during 1951–1965 was 3.6 percentage points higher than the 4 percent growth during the crucial productive years of the Japanese period of 1911–1940.[16]

Professor Jacoby's report ended on an optimistic note that given wise policies and a peaceful international environment "Taiwan could within

15 years achieve the per capita income of an advanced economy today." The per capita income was expected to rise from $160 in 1965 to about $300 per capita by 1980. "This would thrust Free China into the ranks of the economically advanced nations," Prof. Jacoby proudly predicted as if recommending a model student.[17]

The "student" in this case, Taiwan, would prove its mentor wrong. By 1980, Taiwan had grown exponentially with an enterprise-driven economy reaching a per capita income of $2280. Interestingly, in later years, as Taiwan prospered, the ROC government fully repaid the American assistance.

Deterrence and a Defense Treaty

An interesting chronology of events placed Taiwan in an increasingly complex geopolitical position. The Eisenhower Administration came into office in January 1953; by summer there was a truce in Korea, this formally ending the conflict but correspondingly freeing up the People's Republic of China to refocus attention from the Korean peninsula back to Taiwan. As important by May 1954, the French in Vietnam has been vanquished after the epic battle of Dien Bien Phu, not only ending the colonial period but also opening Vietnam to a de facto division, the creation of two states: the communist Democratic Republic of Vietnam (North) and the Republic of Vietnam (South). While Vietnam's division was devised by policymakers as a "temporary step," the reality emerged in which there were two competing Vietnamese states.

The Geneva Peace Conference in 1954 was tasked with a momentous challenge of peace in the Far East. The People's Republic of China was emerging as a serious player. In a *Time* magazine cover story, "Red China's Chou En Lai–Waging War and Talking Peace," the article warned darkly, "If the Russians and Chinese want to settle at Geneva for half of Indo-China, there is a good chance that they can have it." The article suggested that Western governments were conceding parts of the region to the communists.[18]

Sensing a propitious political climate, during 1954 and 1955, the People's Republic of China (PRC) commenced artillery bombardments on the Nationalist held islands of Quemoy and Matsu, two fortress islands just a stone's throw off the Mainland shores. Whether or not these attacks were probes or the prelude to a widespread attack was initially unclear.

What quickly came into focus was Taiwan's vulnerability to large-scale attack by the Chinese communists. John Foster Dulles, the Secretary of State, knew a diplomatic "counterthrust" was necessary to clear the gathering political uncertainty. In the reception rooms of the State Department in Washington, Secretary Dulles and his Nationalist counterpart Foreign Minister George K.C. Yeh concluded the USA/Republic of China Mutual Defense Treaty, signed in December 1954. The Treaty clearly stipulated the defense of Taiwan and the Pescadores islands but significantly not the exposed and vulnerable islands of Quemoy and Matsu. The US Congress later passed the landmark "Formosa Resolution" in January 1955, authorizing the President to "employ the armed forces of the United States as he deems necessary for the specific purpose of security and protecting Formosa and the Pescadores against armed attack."[19]

Secretary Dulles stressed the significance of the Congressional "Formosa Resolution." On 25 January, the resolution was passed by the House of Representatives by a margin of 410 to 3, and within days the Senate by a vote of 83 to 3. Through his deliberate ambiguity toward Quemoy and Matsu, Dulles guaranteed support for both the Mutual Defense Treaty and the Formosa Resolution.[20]

Diplomatic historian F.W. Marks stressed, "Both the Defense Treaty and the Congressional Resolution were the work of the able and adroit Secretary of State John Foster Dulles, whose measured response came amid repeated, but spurned, offers of political concessions to the Chinese communists. The Treaty came with a classic set of caveats since the Secretary felt that if Washington was going to commit itself to a military link with Taipei, it should exercise more control on the ground. Chiang had expected an American guarantee on Quemoy and Matsu to be explicit, while Dulles preferred to be vague."[21]

In a policy statement on Formosa prepared for President Eisenhower, Secretary Dulles was clear: "The security of Taiwan (including the Pescadores) is essential to the best interests of the United States and the Western world. The U.S. as a matter of enlightened self-interest, is resolved to help maintain a Free China Government on Taiwan. This is a fundamental position." The Secretary outlined that American aid to Taiwan over the past five years amounted to $527 million in economic aid and $948 million in military assistance.[22]

Dulles stressed the significance of the 1954 Mutual Defense Treaty with the ROC, "so as to bring its treaty relations with that Republic into harmony with the system of mutual defense treaties linking the U.S. with other countries in the Western Pacific area." He interestingly added,

"The U.S. never considered the retention by Nationalist China of the offshore islands was essential to the U.S. interests." Dulles stated that the USA has also taken the lead in preventing the substitution of the Chinese Communist regime for the Republic of China in the UN.[23]

Rumblings at the UN

As a member of the Allied Big Five during WWII (Britain, China, France, USSR, and the USA), the Republic of China thus was one of the founders of the UN. The Nanking government sent a delegation to San Francisco to help frame the UN Charter. When the Charter went into effect in October 1945, the ROC government by virtue of its founders' status assumed one of the Permanent Five seats on the decision-making Security Council.

Thus, the Nationalists in Nanjing held the China seat at the UN at the end of the WWII and fully four years before Mao's communists conquered the Chinese Mainland. Nationalist China's delegates signed the UN Charter. In the early years of the UN, the ROC's position in the world organization was not a seriously debated issue expect for opposition from the Soviet bloc.

Just weeks before hostilities commenced in Korea, US Secretary of State Dean Acheson reviewed comments by the UN Secretary General Trygve Lie concerning the brewing "China seat" impasse at the UN.

> "The Secretary General states that there no significant progress can be made while members of the United Nations remain divided on the question of Chinese representation ... the present situation in the United Nations does not arise from our position on the question of Chinese representation, but from the refusal of the Soviet Union to accept decisions taken by parliamentary majorities in the various organs of the United Nations."

Dean Acheson stressed, "Their refusal constitutes a boycott of the United Nations and an unwarranted attempt at coercion. We do not like coercion." The Secretary added, "We will accept the decision of any organ of the United Nations made by the necessary majority, and we will not walk out."

Ironically, just weeks later, the Soviet boycott allowed for the Security Council to pass a landmark resolution to safeguard South Korea.[24]

Though the Korean War in 1950 thrust the UN into the headlines, the very fact that the Security Council was able to pass a number of robust enforcement resolutions to defend Korea from the North Korean armed aggression was due to the fact that the Soviets were boycotting the Security Council. Ironically, when quick American diplomatic action called a meeting in the early hours of 25 June, the Soviets were boycotting the Council in deference to the People's Republic of China not having "its rightful seat." Thus, Moscow's powerful veto was not used to block the US draft resolution.

A National Intelligence Estimate (NIE) in August 1957 overviewed the looming diplomatic problem for the ROC. "Given continued U.S. support, the National Government will probably maintain its position on Taiwan, although its international position will deteriorate." It continued, "With U.S. diplomatic support, the Republic of China continues to maintain its formal international position. The Nationalists gained from the hardening of world opinion toward the Bloc because of recent events in Hungary and the Middle East ... pressure, however continues in favor of Communist China's entry into the UN."[25]

The NIE warned ominously,

"The admission of Communist China to the UN would be a serious psychological blow to the National Government. In the Nationalist view it would signify world acceptance of Communist victory in China, U.S. unwillingness or inability to prevent this acceptance and a consequent further weakening of prospects for a Nationalist return ... the long term staying power of the Republic of China will be determined by the policies of the U.S., by developments within Communist China, and by the ability of Nationalist leaders to adjust to life on Taiwan."[26]

On the UN membership issues, a Brooking Institution report stated candidly,

"The fact that the United States recognizes the National Government in Formosa as the legitimate government of China does not resolve the difficulties of the situation. For though a large majority of the members of the United Nations, notably France, the English-speaking British dominions, and all the American republics are in the same camp as the United States, the Chinese Communist regime has been recognized by countries of the Soviet bloc, and by Great Britain, India, Pakistan, Indonesia and a few other states."[27]

Though Brookings added, "The National Government in Formosa has recovered confidence and is engaged with American help in trying to turn Formosa into a model Asian state," the 1954 report warns, "Among the members of the United Nations there is a considerable sentiment in favor of opening the question of which of two Chinese governments should be regarded as representing China." On that question, the report stresses firmly that "public opinion in the United States would not tolerate" admitting the People's Republic of China into the UN.[28]

A political sea change was already taking place at the UN by the mid-1950s. At the onset in 1945, the multinational organization started with 51 members, including of course Allied Big Five from WWII. By 1955, there was the first major membership expansion, which came as the result of serious negotiations and diplomatic "horse trading" between Western states and the Soviet bloc. The moves to expand membership started in 1949 when 12 applications came before the Security Council. In late 1955, the Security Council would subsequently approve 16 states for UN membership, including such former Axis states as Italy, Finland, and Hungary, as well as Albania, Austria, Bulgaria, Cambodia, Ireland, Portugal, and Spain. Significantly, the "package deal" expansion did not include applicants the Republic of Korea (South Korea), not the Republic of Vietnam (South Vietnam). On 14 December, the General Assembly approved the 16 new UN member states.[29]

Given that by 1955, the world body had a wider and more politically diverse membership, 76 states, correspondingly new pressures would come to bear on Taipei's position. The Annual vote in General Assembly on the "China seat" soon became a feature of the political landscape. Throughout the 1950s, despite pressures from the Soviets, deft American diplomacy kept the China representation issue from coming to a formal General Assembly vote. From 1962 onward, the "Representation of China" issue would hang like a storm cloud over the Assembly. In September 1962, the Soviets asked that the agenda item, "Restoration of the lawful rights of the People's Republic of China in the United Nations," be included on the agenda. Between 22 and 30 October, in what would become an annual ritual, seven meetings of the Assembly presented the point and counterpoint to Moscow's proposal. On 30 October, the Soviet draft resolution was defeated by a vote of 42 to 56 with 12 abstentions. Besides the Soviets and traditional East bloc states, the Russians were backed by India, Indonesia, Iran, and surprisingly the UK. Opposition came from the USA, Australia, Nationalist China, and a wide swath of West European and Latin American states. Nonetheless, Moscow would not stop its initiative after one setback. Moreover, with the UN on the verge of an expanded membership in the wake of African decolonization, the winds of change would begin to shift on the shores of the East River.[30]

Quemoy and Matsu Redux

Though on slow simmer since 1954, the offshore islands of Quemoy and Matsu were thrust back into the headlines in August 1958. Chinese Communist forces initiated a massive artillery bombardment of Quemoy and later tightened a blockade on the island. As President Dwight D. Eisenhower wrote in his Memoirs, *Waging Peace*, "While the Formosa proclaimed an American determination to defend that island, and the neighboring Pescadores, an attack on the offshore islands would justify our military participation only if, I as President should judge the attack to be a preliminary to an assault on Formosa."[31]

The Chinese Nationalist Navy, with American advisors, broke the blockade with daring seaborne resupply missions, while the Free Chinese Air Force flying its Sabre jets maintained air superiority in the Formosa Straits.

After two months of bombardment, Beijing paused. As President Eisenhower wrote, "The Chinese Communists now suddenly announced that they would fire on Nationalist convoys only on odd days of the month, and would permit the Chinese Nationalists to resupply the offshore garrisons on even numbered days." Eisenhower joked, "I wonder if we were in a Gilbert and Sullivan war?"

He added, "Thus the crisis passed."[32]

John Foster Dulles visited Taipei to meet with Chiang Kai-shek and to convince the ROC leader to reject the use of force if at all possible in seeking the return to the Mainland. The Dulles/Chiang communiqué stated that the mission of the ROC "resided in the minds and hearts of the Chinese people," and that "The principal means of achieving that mission would be the implantation of the three principles of Dr. Sun Yat-sen; nationalism, democracy, and social welfare, and not necessarily the use of force." Shortly after Dulles left Taipei, Beijing declared a de facto ceasefire.[33]

What could have been a trigger to a renewed Far East conflict between the USA and China instead became a footnote of history. When President Eisenhower made a visit to Taiwan in 1960, he was welcomed by Beijing with a massive bombardment of Quemoy and Matsu. Indeed, during the memorable Presidential TV debates in the 1960 election, both Vice President Richard Nixon and his Democratic contender Senator John F. Kennedy sparred over this issue. Into the 1970s, Quemoy and Matsu were still locked in the Even Day Odd Day routine with shelling of the islands not with high explosives but with propaganda leaflets. The Nationalist counter-batteries responded with loudspeakers, popular music, and balloons with packages of leaflets, food, and radios for the Mainland.

Though all was soon reasonably quiet in Quemoy, the crisis underscored a subtle but not acknowledged shift in the Nationalist policy from a bellicose "Re-conquer the Mainland" to a tacit realization of the reality that Taipei was not just the "temporary capital" of the ROC government, but in fact their home. Though disproportionate ROC military spending still focused on an epic re-conquest of Mainland China, the reality was shifting politically. Taiwan was safe across the Formosa Straits and behind the US defense Treaty.

ROC as "Free China"

In parallel to American military and economic assistance, the ROC government was supported by a well-oiled political operation in Washington which sought to build and keep bi-partisan support for Chiang's KMT government. Often called the "China Lobby," the effort during the 1950s would build strong bi-partisan political support for Taiwan and in turn protect the ROC's island redoubt. In 1953, a group known as "The Committee for One Million Against the Admission of Communist China to the United Nations" was one such group of a larger American support network for Free China often known as the "China Lobby." Indeed, "for eighteen years, from 1953 to 1971, 'The Committee for One Million,' and its successor 'The Committee of One Million,'" comprised a key element of the China Lobby in American politics. Members of Congress, most notably Walter Judd (R/Minnesota), played a strong role in supporting Taiwan. As one account argues, "Irrespective of its linguistic origins on the left,

---

ROC Pavilion at the 1964 World's Fair The Republic of China Pavilion in the 1964–1965, New York World's Fair presented a lavish Chinese architectural showcase illustrating "an exposition of art, culture, and modern progress." Historic treasures from China's earlier dynasties, wall and ceiling carvings recreating the style of an Imperial palace, as well as exhibits of contemporary Land Reform and economic development, comprised one of the Fair's most popular international pavilions.

> Prominently located near the iconic steel *Unisphere Globe*, which remains to this day, the opulent red and gold ROC Pavilion was much more than a lavish exhibit. Given that the still-isolated People's Republic of China was barred from the Fair, the pavilion allowed Taiwan to stress its legitimacy as well as project its role as both the legitimate heir to and custodian of Chinese civilization.
> *Source*: Official Guide/New York World's Fair 1964–1965. New York: Time Life Books, 1964, pp. 112, 166

'China Lobby' became a convenient expression for characterizing Chiang Kai-shek's supporters on the right."[34]

Military spending placed a burden on Taiwan's economy. "The military forces of Free China were among the largest in the world in proportion to population," wrote Prof. Jacoby, adding, "they comprised about 600,000 men, equal to 7.6 percent of Taiwan's civilian population of 7.8 million at the end of 1951 and 4.9 percent of its population of 12,100,000 at the end of 1964." Taiwan's military expenditures were also among the world's highest in proportion to GNP. Between 1951 and 1965, military spending consistently averaged 9–11 percent of GNP. Such spending, according to Prof. Jacoby, comprised between 70 and 80 percent of all national government expenditures. The outlays were apart from the large US Military Assistance Program (MAP) to Taiwan which consisted of weapons and military hardware.[35]

By the late 1960s, Taiwan's military spending dropped marginally to 7.6 percent of GNP in 1968, reflecting actual spending of $300 million. In that same period, the PRC spending was still an amazing 9 percent of GNP with an annual outlay of $7 billion. Military forces totaled 555,000 out of a population of 13.7 million people.[36]

During this period, 1951–1971, Taiwan's rebuilding and national security remained paramount for the embattled ROC government. Growing economic and educational advancement were nonetheless producing results and the island was becoming increasingly prosperous. Security was ensured by the US Mutual Defense Treaty. Politically speaking, Taiwan was governed by an authoritarian system where the Nationalist/Kuomintang party (KMT) held the levers of power and government, not unlike many other East Asian countries. Yet, the ROC government's dream of reconquering the Mainland added a messianic vision to the debate and so much of Taiwan's politics were still viewed through this prism.

In July 1971, half a world away in Washington, President Richard Nixon stunned the nation by announcing he would be visiting communist China the following year. The surprise statement, which signaled a major shift in US China policy, sought to "seek normalization of relations between the two countries." The move in the midst of China's own *Cultural Revolution* and the ongoing Vietnam War hit many Far Eastern capitals, such as Tokyo and Taipei, like a lightning bolt. Though President Nixon advised that "our actions in seeking a new relationship with the People's Republic of China, will not be at the expense of our old friends"; in reality, the USA was beginning to recalibrate and possibly shift its policy, signaling a new East wind was blowing.[37]

The UN "China Seat" Showdown

During early 1971, it was becoming increasingly obvious that the annual China representation vote at the UN could swing against the US position. Even some firm European allies were suggesting a "dual representation" for the two Chinas, and indeed the concept was gaining traction in the State Department. Between 1961 and 1970, the annual General Assembly debate had failed to gain the two-thirds majority to pass a resolution ousting the ROC. By 1970, through a resolution passed by 66 votes to 52 to keep Taiwan in the Assembly, a sea change was emerging.[38]

The *Nixon Shock* of 15 July, regarding a political rapprochement with Peking, had triggered seismic political recalculations globally from the Far East to the East River in New York where the UN would take up the China representation issue. Japan was particularly nervous over the political ramifications of the policy shift.

On 2 August, Secretary of State William Rogers announced that the USA would support a "dual representation solution" to Chinese representation at the upcoming UN session. Secretary Rogers's announcement marked a switch for American that Washington had dropped its opposition to seating the People's Republic of China. The position reflected "a climate of opinion which had developed in the General Assembly in favor of seating the People's Republic of China." In a larger sense, the dual representation position reflected "the Nixon Administration's continuing effort to adjust to the reality of Mainland China without severing American ties with the Government on Taiwan."[39]

The die was cast. The 26th General Assembly of the UN began its rites of autumn and the debate over the Chinese representation. On 18 October, the Assembly opened its annual consideration of the "China seat." Agenda item 93, "Restoration of the Lawful Rights of the People's Republic of China in the United Nations," witnessed a spirited weeklong debate on an Albanian draft resolution. The Albanian delegate stated, "It is more essential than ever to give that great and powerful socialist country its rightful place in this organization and to expel the Chiang Kai-shek clique."[40] In a series of often shrill statements, delegates from the People's Republic of Yemen opined, "The U.S. with its imperialist policy, has imposed the Chiang Kai-shek clique on the UN as the representatives of China for more than twenty years, ignoring the real representatives of China and its great people."[41]

On Monday, 25 October, delegations heard the closing arguments on what diplomats knew would be a *fait accompli* in the Assembly. American Ambassador George H.W. Bush presented the closing arguments,

> "The issue is not the seating of the People's Republic of China in the UN. In fact, for the first time in history there is something close to unanimity behind the proposition that it is time for the People's Republic to take its seat in the United Nations, including its seat as a permanent member of the Security Council. That is a major historic development. It is not an issue in the UN anymore."

Torn between traditional US political support for Taipei and the dawn of better relations with Beijing, Ambassador Bush strove for political damage control, "This is the issue: Shall we expel forthwith the Republic of China from the United Nations, or shall it continue to be represented here? That is the heart of the matter ... the ROC should not and must not be deprived of its United Nations representation." The Ambassador offered an alternative plan, which, as Bush said, would "retain the ROC in the UN while seating the PRC in both the General Assembly and Security Council. It reflects plain facts who governs in Taiwan as well as who governs the Chinese Mainland."[42]

The Chinese representation question was decided on at literally the 11th hour. A weary General Assembly voted 76 to 35, with 17 abstentions. The East Bloc and Third World, along with American allies such as Britain, Canada, and France, backed Beijing being seated. Along with the USA, key opponents included Australia, Japan, and New Zealand. Greece,

Jordan, and Spain abstained. With the adoption of the Albanian resolution #2758 (XXVI), many Third-World delegates literally danced in the aisles when the meeting ended at 11:25 p.m.

The American *dual representation* draft was never voted on. Taiwan's delegates withdrew from the cavernous Assembly Hall before the PRC was seated.[43]

Following the vote, Taiwan faced political aftershocks in the UN system: the ROC was soon expelled from UN specialized agencies such as the International Civil Aviation Organization (ICAO), the International Atomic Energy Agency (IAEA), UN Educational Scientific and Cultural Organization (UNESCO), and the World Health Organization (WHO).[44]

The ROC's UN ouster was the first of three major diplomatic setbacks for Taipei within the year; in February, the Nixon visit to Mainland China changed the political calculus of American China policy. Later in the year, Japan, Australia, and New Zealand would recognize Beijing. The diplomatic setback on the East River in New York presaged the political East Wind which was blowing.

Notes

1. Foreign Relations of the United States (FRUS), 1950 Vol. VII/Korea, (Washington, DC: GPO, 1976), pp. 162–164.
2. US Department of State (USDS) "American Foreign Policy 1950–1955, Basic Documents" (Washington, DC: GPO 1957), p. 2468.
3. The UN Security Council met in the early morning hours on Sunday 25 June. Given that the Soviets were boycotting the Council in protest to Nationalist China holding the Council's China seat, American Ambassador Warren Austin was able to quickly marshal support, avoid a Soviet veto, and pass a few resolutions such as the landmark enforcement resolution #83 (1950) which recommended "members of the United Nations furnish such assistance to the Republic of Korea as may be necessary to repel the armed attack and restore international peace and security in the area." The Council equally established a unified military command, authorized the use of the UN flag for operations, and requested the Council designate a force commander. General Douglas MacArthur was appointed force commander.
4. "Turning of the Tide in Korea and the Meeting of "a New Foe." United Nations Bulletin Vol. 9, no. 10, 10 November 1950, pp. 528–529.

5. Ibid., p. 534.
6. FRUS, 1950 Vol. VI/East Asia and the Pacific, (Washington, DC: GPO: 1976), pp. 529–531.
7. FRUS, 1951 Vol. VII/The China Area, (Washington, DC: GPO: 1976), p. 1859.
8. Ibid., p. 1597.
9. Paul K. T. Sih, Editor, Taiwan in Modern Times, (New York: St. John's University Press, 1973), pp. 491–492.
10. Ibid., pp. 411–412.
11. *China Yearbook* 1972–1973. (Taipei: China Publishing, 1973), p. 218.
12. Neil Jacoby, "An Evaluation of U.S. Economic Aid to Free China 1951–1965," Agency for International Development/Bureau of Far East Aid, (Washington, DC: 1966), pp. 21–22.
13. Ibid., p. 23.
14. Ibid., p. 30.
15. Ibid., p. 42.
16. Ibid., p. 48.
17. Ibid., p. 84.
18. Time, 10 May 1954, Vol. 63, No. 19, p. 28.
19. Time, 13 December 1954, Vol. 64, No. 24, p. 11. USDS "American Foreign Policy" 1957, 2 pp. 2486–2487.
20. Frederick W. Marks. Power and Peace: The Diplomacy of John Foster Dulles. (Westport, CT: Praeger, 1993), pp. 81–82.
21. Ibid., pp. 81–84.
22. FRUS, 1955–1957, Vol. 2/The China Area, pp. 455–457.
23. Ibid., p. 457.
24. US Mission to the UN/Press Release, No. 881, 7 June 1950.
25. Foreign Relations, 1955–1957, Vol. 3/The China Area, pp. 586, 589.
26. Ibid., p, 592.
27. Major Problems of United States Foreign Policy 1954. Brookings Institution (Washington, DC: 1954), p. 314.
28. Ibid., p. 316.
29. "Membership Debated Again," United Nations Bulletin, Vol. VII, no. 2, 15 July 1949, pp. 89–92; Yearbook of the United Nations 1955, Department of Public Information, (United Nations, New York, 1956): pp. 22–29. The full roster of the new members included *Albania, Austria, Bulgaria, Cambodia, Ceylon, Finland,*

Hungary, Ireland, Italy, Jordan, Laos, Libya, Nepal, Portugal, Romania, and Spain.
30. Yearbook of the United Nations 1962 Department of Public Information (United Nations, New York, 1964): pp. 114–117.
31. Dwight D. Eisenhower. Waging Peace 1956–1961. (Doubleday, NY: Garden City, New York, 1965), p. 294.
32. Ibid., p. 304. For a fascinating account of Quemoy and Matsu in the period following the ceasefire, the book *The Odd Day* by DeWitt Copp and Marshall Peck (William Morrow: New York, 1962), offers a rare glimpse of the forgotten period.
33. Kenneth Young. Negotiating with the Chinese Communists: The American Experience 1953–1967. (McGraw Hill: New York, 1968), pp. 197–198.
34. Stanley Bachrack. *The Committee of One Million; "China Lobby" Politics 1953–1971*. (New York: Columbia University Press, 1976), pp. 4–7. This book presents a detailed account of the origins, support, and focus of the "China Lobby" which comprised an informal group of Congressmen and policy officials and key Republican and Democratic supporters of Taiwan.
35. Op. cit. "U.S. Economic Aid to Free China," p. 35.
36. The Military Balance 1969–1970. (Institute for Strategic Studies: London, 1969), pp. 42, 58.
37. Nixon Address to the Nation 15 July 1971, Nixonfoundation.org
38. United Nations General Assembly (UNGA) Plenary, 20 November 1970.
39. FRUS, 1969–1976 Vol. V United Nations 1969–1972, (Washington, DC: GPO, 2004), p. 913. What became known as the Nixon Shock resulting from the surprise announcement that the President would visit the PRC was viewed as a particular jolt to relations with Japan. Washington's moves had not been properly explained and cleared with Tokyo, thus causing a fear that the USA would "dump Japan" at some point in the future.
40. UNGA/Plenary, 18 October 1971, pp. 1–3.
41. UNGA/Plenary, 20 October 1971, p. 5.
42. UNGA/Plenary, 25 October 1971, pp. 11–14.
43. UNGA/Plenary, 25 October 1971, p. 14.
44. Yearbook of the United Nations 1971 Volume 25, Office of Public Information (United Nations: New York, 1974), pp. 134–135.

CHAPTER 4

The Republic of China 1972–1992

The diplomatic *tsunami* swamping Taiwan in the aftermath of the UN debacle posed one of the biggest political setbacks to the ROC since Chiang Kai-shek's forces fled the Mainland. In the year leading up to the loss of the ROC's UN seat, key countries such as Canada, Ethiopia, Italy, and Iran switched recognition to Beijing. In a matter of months after the UN vote, former allies such as Argentina and Japan switched recognition. Between 25 October 1971 and the end of 1972, the ROC had lost 25 countries, including West Germany, Australia, and New Zealand.[1]

The Nixon visit to Beijing in February 1972 presented a political watershed in US–China relations as much a masterpiece of political choreography in which the implacable anti-communist American President and the Chinese communist leadership forged fledgling links but created indelible political perceptions.

Central to the visit was the Shanghai communiqué in which both governments stated that there is but one China but with a decidedly different interpretation as to the specifics. The USA affirmed what had been a geographical truism, "The United States acknowledges that all Chinese on either side of the Taiwan Strait acknowledge there is but one China, and that Taiwan is part of China. The U.S. government does not challenge that position." Washington's position stressed "the peaceful settlement of the Taiwan question by the Chinese themselves." The Shanghai

Communiqué did not establish the legal status of Taiwan nor did the USA side accept Beijing's claims to sovereign jurisdiction over the island. In the very same communiqué, the PRC insisted that "the government of the People's Republic of China is the sole legal government of China; Taiwan is a province of China."[2] It bears mention that bilateral communiqués are not considered legally binding in US constitutional law, a point the PRC seems to have overlooked.

The document was drafted between Henry Kissinger, the president National Security Advisor, and Chou Enlai. According to Kissinger, in his book *Diplomacy*, "In February 1972, Nixon signed the Shanghai Communique, which was to provide a road map for Sino-American relations for the next decade." He added, however, "The Communique had an unprecedented feature: More than half of it was devoted to stating the conflicting views of the two sides on ideology, international affairs, Vietnam and Taiwan."[3]

As Kissinger advised, "The Shanghai Communique and the diplomacy leading up to it enabled the Nixon Administration to put in place what it called, perhaps somewhat grandiloquently, a new structure of peace. As soon as America's opening to China was announced, the pattern of international relations changed dramatically."[4]

Following the Nixon visit, "Mao and Zhou Enlai abandoned their opposition to America's alliance in the Asia-Pacific," advised Dr. Michael Yahuda of the London School of Economics. "Thus Mao came to appreciate the significance of the Tokyo–Washington axis. ... Mao and Zhou Enlai also tacitly supported the U.S. military presence in the Philippines, Thailand and even South Korea," Yahuda added.[5]

Significantly, though the Nixon trip to China did not open diplomatic relations between Washington and Beijing, nor did it affect the longstanding US defense Treaty commitments to Taiwan, the visit changed political expectations and calculations on both sides of the Taiwan Strait. A noticeable sea change in relations followed.

Taipei was facing diplomatic isolation if not political suffocation. Though diplomatically isolated, Taiwan in the 1970s and the increasingly confident Taiwan of the 1980s emerged as an economically vibrant player on the global economic stage.

On the governmental side, Chiang Ching-kuo was appointed Premier in May 1972, opening a new era. Ching-kuo, president Chiang's oldest son, was bequeathed a position of power by his father. The symbolism was clear;

Chiang Kai-shek, the aging mandarin and remaining WWII leader, was grudgingly preparing a transition. To be sure since fleeing the Mainland in 1949, the KMT government was seeking a refuge and a last-ditch redoubt. Politics on Taiwan in the early years were national/security oriented and predictably defensive. The authoritarian political system, which characterized KMT rule, however, was subtlety and later significantly challenged by the impressive socio-economic changes on the island. Land Reform through the *Land to the Tiller* movement and growing industrialization would serve as catalysts for political change.

The ROC government structures on Taiwan mirrored the system on the pre-war Mainland. This was, after all, at least in the 1950s, seen as a government in exile with Taipei as China's *provisional capital*, pending reunification. The mantra of reconquering the Mainland or *Guangfu Dalu* reflected ROC government policy into the late 1970s.

At the same time, the ROC still adhered to a blend of Confucian social values mixed with modernity in the economic sphere.

GOVERNMENT STRUCTURES

The Republic of China government was established in 1912 but in its current form was guided by the Constitution of 1946. Just over a year after VJ day in 1945, a Constituent Assembly met in Nanking to adopt the new Constitution. That constitution, allowing for a five-branch system, devised by Dr. Sun Yat-sen, combines the cabinet and presidential systems of government. Indeed, the highest organ of the ROC government was the National Assembly, last elected in 1947 and whose 2961 delegates represented all China. Though the National Assembly fills roughly the same role as the US electoral college in electing the president, the body also has the right of recall and referendum, and remains the only organ of government with the powers to alter the boundaries of the country.[6]

The presidency is the next level of government. In Taiwan's early days, Chiang Kai-shek was re-elected by the National Assembly in 1972, to serve his fifth (and final) six-year term. As chief of state, the president holds significant powers in the foreign and domestic arena. Until the early 1990s, the ROC President was not directly elected by the populace.

The Executive Yuan, serving as the administration of government, came into being originally in 1928. The Executive Yuan is the highest administrative organ of the nation.

The Premier takes responsibility for the day-to-day functions and formalities of government. Government Ministries and their respective Ministers such as the Ministry of the Interior, Ministry of Foreign Affairs, Ministry of National Defense, Ministry of Education, and Ministry of Economic Affairs, among others, are responsible to the Primier and this level of government.[7]

The Legislative Yuan forms the law-making branch of the government. An elected body, the Yuan, saw its first elections on the Mainland in 1948, with 760 members elected. But given the government loss of the Mainland and relocation to Taiwan, the legislative branch during Taiwan's early years became another casualty of the divide. As of August 1972, the number of legislators totaled 420. Only in 1969 were there fresh elections for 11 new members representing Taiwan. In effect, the large and unwieldy Legislative Yuan, despite its considerable power in the budgetary and law-making arena, and its twice annual sessions from February to May and September to December, remained a quaint anachronism.[8]

The Judicial Yuan, the Examination Yuan, and the Control Yuan remain the other three branches of the ROC government. The Examination Yuan, whose roots date to ancient China, is responsible for civil service examinations and government recruitment. The civil service examination process, a mainstay of both dynastic China and refurbished for the modern era, is the function of this branch. Equally, the Control Yuan, another unique function with roots in ancient China, serves as an oversight agency to all levels of government and leadership and legislation. The powers of censure and corrective measures are within the purview of the Control Yuan.[9]

Dr. Sun Yat-sen, the founder of the Chinese Republic, set forth his political doctrine in the *Three Principles of the People* (San Min Chu I), which represented and still serve as the guiding principles for the ROC: Nationalism, Democracy, and Livelihood/Well Being. Sun's view of Nationalism meant liberating the Chinese nation from foreign invasion and oppression. Democracy stood for the rights of the people as structured in the government with five powers: Executive, Legislative, Judicial, Examination, and Control. Livelihood/well-being would affect the freedom and happiness of the people, with an equalization of land ownership. The *Min-sheng*, the people's Livelihood, a concept of well-being, was perhaps the most elusive.[10]

The People's Livelihood principle would come into fruition on Taiwan in ways few, even in the government, would have expected. The extraordinary socio-economic growth rates, based on a foundation of growing educational opportunities, hard work, and a positive can-do spirit of a growing class of small entrepreneurs, would ensure dramatic and sustained growth rates.

After rebuilding agriculture on a firm and fair basis, the Taiwan government began to stress manufacturing both for import substitution and for export reasons. Manufacturing share of the GDP rose from 10.8 percent in 1952 to 25.6 percent in 1971. Machinery, electrical machinery, and appliances made up a large share of the output.[11]

The textile industry would play a significant role in both industrialization and exports too. Though textiles growth increased from 7 percent during the 1954–1971 period, the textile market share surged to 27 percent during 1966–1971. Indeed, "the rapid expansion of labor-intensive light manufacturing up until 1970 particularly of the food processing, textile, and electrical machinery industries, characterized a specific pattern of industrialization in Taiwan," according to Prof. John C.H. Fei. Yet, in the period 1971–1979, these industries saw a smaller share of manufacturing, being replaced by skill-intensive industries such as petrochemicals, metals, and machinery.[12]

The impressive growth of Taiwan's export sector was soon based on manufacturing; exports of agricultural product fell from 92 percent in 1952 to 9 percent in 1979, while industrial products surged from 8 percent to 91 percent during the same period. Foreign trade had become a mainstay of the economy as the *Taiwan Success Story* recounts. With exports of $16 billion and imports of 14.8 billion in 1979, the Republic of China became the 21st largest trading country worldwide and the 9th largest partner of the USA.[13]

"The trade dependency of the Taiwan economy grew significantly over the past three decades," states *Taiwan Success Story*, "the percentage of exports in GNP increased from 9 percent in 1952 to 49 percent in 1980; that of imports from 15 percent to 49 percent." American aid financed many imports in the early years. Equally, the USA became the largest market for Taiwan's products standing at almost 42 percent in 1971 and 35 percent in 1979.[14]

Although public enterprises predominated in the early years of the ROC's return to Taiwan, the government pursued plans to transfer state-owned enterprises to the private sector. Of the 1971 industrial production, 80 percent came from the private sector as compared with 44 percent in 1952.[15]

An increasingly export-oriented economy was driven by a unique Taiwan invention: the Export Processing Zone (EPZ). The Kaohsiung EPZ, opened in 1966, incorporated the advantages of a free trade zone and industrial district through a series of tax and investment incentives. By the early 1970s, the Kaohsiung EPZ had over 160 projects with an investment of $48 million. Employment totaled 44,620 while exports from the site were valued at $156 million in 1971. Other EPZs were set up throughout the island.[16]

Such zones, later successfully copied in Mainland China, became an engine of export success.

Significantly, in 1973, a year after the devastating diplomatic setbacks, and the initial jolt of the oil crisis, Taiwan's economy nonetheless grew at an impressive 11.9 percent.[17]

At this juncture, Taiwan was making the complicated transition from a developing to a more developed economy. Manufactured goods and services were produced from privately owned firms many of which were inspired by the island's entrepreneurial business class.

Economic Jumpstart

Nonetheless, the public sector still held a heavy hand in certain industries. The Ten Major Construction Projects were symbolic of the classic government economic intervention model favored in many countries. Planned during the economic gloom of the 1973–1974 energy crisis, the projects represented a bold step by Premier Chiang Ching-kuo's new and still untested government. The projects stressed infrastructural development: a north–south freeway, port upgrades, a nuclear power plant, petrochemicals, and building the China Shipbuilding and China Steel complexes in Kaohsiung. As Taiwan's air transportation links had outgrown the old Taipei Sungshan Airport, a new Airport was constructed at Taoyuan. As of 1975, the ten projects cost $6.6 billion. For example, the north–south freeway, a 235-mile highway linking Keelung in the north with Kaohsiung in the south, cost $1.2 billion.[18]

Still, despite notable economic development, Taiwan in the mid- to late 1970s had an air of unmistakable political uncertainty. Both the UN setback and the collapse of South Vietnam in April 1975 offered stark proof that Taiwan was on both the political and possibly the military defensive. The events in Indochina, while not connected to Taiwan's sovereignty, reminded the island of its precarious existence vis-à-vis the People's

Republic. Moreover, Washington's perceptible political shift toward a relationship with Beijing was viewed as a corresponding tilt away from Taipei.

"Between 1963 and mid-1975 countries recognizing the ROC dropped from 66 to 26. While the PRC went from 50 to 112," advised Prof. Bellows.[19]

Diplomatic relations with so many of the ROC's close and traditional allies fell like dominos in the wake of the UN debacle. Even in the 1960s, Taiwan hosted some high-profile diplomatic visits, including US President Dwight Eisenhower, King Bhumibol of Thailand, President Park Chung-hee of South Korea, and many African heads of state.

During this period, Chiang Kai-shek remained the undisputed leader of Taiwan, though official portraits viewed him as a major force in the Far East. One such hagiographic account puts it succinctly, "Chiang Kai-shek is a ranking statesman of the world. President Chiang is leading the Chinese toward recovery of the Chinese Mainland. His counsel is sought by the great and the near-great democratic lands everywhere."[20]

President Chiang passed away on 5 April 1975, coincidently the traditional Chinese day of *Ching-ming* or tomb-sweeping day. Chiang's death represented the passing of the last of the Allied "Big Five" leaders from WWII. "The Republic of China and the rest of the free world made their last tearful farewell April 16 to the man who first unified China and then guided its destiny for 50 years, the late President Chiang Kai-shek," wrote the government journal *Free China Weekly*. The article described the funeral in the massive Sun Yat-sen Hall, which was attended by many foreign envoys, including US Vice President Nelson Rockefeller.[21]

> *Sun Yat-sen Memorial Hall and Chiang Kai-shek Memorial and Cultural Centre* Back in the early 1970s, Sun Yat-sen Memorial Hall opened in Taipei. The large Chinese-style architecture structure honored the revolutionary and founder of the Republic of China. Sun is actually buried in Nanking, China. The grand edifice was part of the KMT government's efforts to honor historical figures and instill patriotism while at the same time providing the still gritty and developing city of Taipei with functional modern architectural structures. The hall was used as both a museum and a cultural center. In 1975, the Complex was the site of Chiang Kai-shek's funeral. Currently, the Hall hosts the Golden Horse Film

> Festival Awards. The Hall is usually seen from the sky, which is to say from the nearby observatory of the iconic Taipei 101 skyscraper, which towers over Taipei.
>
> The Chiang Kai-shek Memorial Hall is part of an immense complex built in the late 1970s after the president's death. Constructed in the traditional Chinese architecture, the marble Hall is approached by staircases of 89 steps, each representing a year of Chiang's life. The Hall hosts a Museum, library, and impressive antechamber with a sitting statue of the late president. The glistening marble building's octagonal roof of blue tiles reaches 250 feet! The Hall is flanked by two equally impressive Chinese buildings, the National Opera House and the National Concert Hall. The plaza connecting these three structures is known as Liberty Square. The complex can be described as nothing less than grandiose.
>
> *Source*: orientalarchitecture.com

Unquestionably, Chiang's rule on Taiwan represented an authoritarian, some would say paternalistic, hand politically while at the same time exhibiting a surprisingly reformist view toward social and economic development. Land Reform and the widening of educational opportunities were building blocks to the extraordinary economic expansion which would soon follow. Chiang had learned his lesson with the loss of the Mainland to Mao's communists, and was not going to repeat any mistakes on Taiwan.

In early 1975, East Asia was in transition. The Indochina wars were coming to a conclusion with the communist takeovers in Cambodia and Vietnam. The USA was openly courting a new relationship with the People's Republic. With the passing of Chiang, a figure who was both a confidant of Dr. Sun Yat-sen and a significant player in most events since the founding of the Republic in 1912, Taiwan was facing untested leadership with the transition to new President Yen Chia-kan.

From a geopolitical perspective, the Soviet Union was strategically ascendant and People's China was being viewed as a counterweight to Moscow's growing military power. Equally, the USA was in shock over the loss of Indochina and off balance politically in the aftermath of the Watergate scandal and the resignation of President Richard M. Nixon in 1974.

Though the short-tenured Ford Administration showed a surprising level of support for Taiwan, change was in the air. Being in Taiwan in the aftermath of the Indochina debacle, I can vividly recall the political angst over American intentions and reliability. Though diplomatic relations were still strong, there was the unmistakable feeling that the USA was clearly tilting its policies from Taiwan to the Mainland. Even as a student, the inevitable question would be, "what would America do if ...?"

The Carter Administration would change many comfortable perceptions in the Pacific. According to Prof. Yahuda, "His Administration's early initiatives in Asia did not inspire confidence in its strategic sense of purpose ... additionally the Administration agonized openly about whether to treat the two communist giants equally and about whether to play the 'China card' by supplying China with arms and deepening relations whenever the Soviet Union was judged to have behaved aggressively."[22]

THE "CHINA CARD"

Without question, Carter's tough Polish-born National Security advisor Zbigniew Brzezinski was a strong disciple of playing China off against a resurgent and military rising Soviet Union. He was not alone. There was a growing consensus both in Washington and in many West European capitals, that the "China Card" was the West's silver bullet in any possible confrontation with Moscow. Thus, the political "China fever" of the early 1970s had morphed into a comfortable strategic rationalization of the "China Card" whereby the People's Republic would in effect become allied with the West against the Soviets.

"A major issue in the minds of China-watchers around the world was the future of Taiwan," wrote James Lilly, the CIA's top China analyst, adding, "Specifically what would happen to Taiwan in the context of an agreement between the U.S. and China to exchange embassies in their respective countries?" He added, "Within the Carter Administration, Brzezinski had taken over China policy from Secretary of State Cyrus Vance and by 1978 dominated the making of China policy in a fashion not unlike that of his predecessor Henry Kissinger. Brzezinski's hard-charging anti-Soviet approach led him to focus on the geopolitical significance of the People's Republic of China."[23]

Dr. Brzezinski's enchantment with playing the "China Card" had as its political component the normalization of diplomatic relations between Washington and Beijing. What started during the Nixon visit in February 1972 as the *Long March* to better US/PRC ties, ended ten days before Christmas 1978 with Carter's announcement that the USA would break relations with the ROC, terminate its Mutual Defense Treaty with Taiwan, remove remaining American forces from the island, and thus open de jure diplomatic relations with the People's Republic of China, effective 1 January 1979.

Carter's announcement came at 9 p.m., Friday 15 December, just before the Christmas recess, precisely to avoid a Congressional confrontation which would have likely been bi-partisan. But, because there was no consultation with Congress, the legislative branch, feeling spurned, reacted. According to James Lilley,

> "A balance to our relationship with Taiwan and mainland China was restored when both houses of Congress passed the Taiwan Relations Act (TRA) in April 1979. Having been shut out of the normalization process, Congress weighed in on the side of Taiwan, in a measured and bi-partisan fashion. Passed 339–50 in the House and 85–4 in the Senate, the Taiwan Relations Act wrote into law security guarantees for Taiwan that were nearly as strong as those contained in the terminated Mutual Defense Treaty."[24]

Interestingly, just days after the announced switch of recognition, Michael Oksenberg, a staffer of the National Security Council, visited former President Richard Nixon for a two-hour conversation at San Clemente. In a report to Brzezinski, the former President was not worried about Taiwan's future. Nixon noted, "Taiwan will survive. There is no problem here. Terminating the Defense Treaty had to occur. Taiwan can defend itself. But this is an emotional issue." The former President's main concern dealt with the impact on US allies: "This is the real concern." To terminate a defense treaty could sow seeds of doubt about us, particularly in Asia. "As a result of this decision, the President cannot make any weak moves in the foreseeable future. For whether this move is weak or not, the termination of our relations with Taiwan will be seen as such."[25]

The American shift from Taipei to Beijing became a *fait accompli* couched in the strategic hopes that the "China Card" would shield the West from the Soviets and that the China Market would be a boon for US commerce. Part of America's enchantment with China dealt with the soon expected bottom line of economic gain.

Shortly after normalization of relations, China's paramount leader Deng Xiaoping toured the USA not so much as a victory lap, but rather as a learning mission. It was Deng after all, earlier persecuted and humiliated by the hardline Maoists, whose pragmatism would allow China's extraordinary economic opening in 1978. Yet, Deng's military misjudgment in "teaching Vietnam a lesson" backfired as the battle-hardened Vietnamese army bloodied China in a short but sharp conflict. Given the southern front with Vietnam, supporting the toppled Beijing-backed Khmer Rouge regime in Cambodia, and trying to restart a still moribund Mainland economy, Deng Xiaoping had little time to focus directly on Taiwan.

Yet, there was a shift in Beijing's once predictable rhetoric.

Notably on 1 January 1979, the day Washington opened diplomatic relations with Peking, the National People's Congress addressed a "Message to Our Taiwan Compatriots." The statement offered a policy to peacefully reunify the Chinese motherland. Such seemingly conciliatory statements contrasted sharply with the PRC's longtime threats to "liberate" Taiwan by force if necessary. By September 1981, the NPC sent a follow-up "greetings to Taiwan Compatriots" which promised Taiwan would become "a special administrative region which could retain its armed forces. Taiwan's current socio/economic system will remain unchanged." In September 1982, Deng Xiaoping proclaimed his signature concept of "one country, two systems," *yiguo liangze*. The concept of "one country, two systems," which would also be extended to Hong Kong, was nervously viewed by the government in Taipei.[26]

Domestic Opposition Emerges

Besides setbacks in the international arena, Taiwan was feeling domestic jolts as well.

By late 1978, non-KMT candidates were competing in elections. These *tangwei* candidates won 19 percent of the newly created National Assembly seats. "This election breakthrough signaled the advance of Taiwan's democracy," adds Dr. Ramon Myers, adding, "These '*tangwei*' politicians were born in Taiwan of parents who strongly identified with the island's culture and language and had lived for one or more generations in Taiwan. Although critical of the KMT's unfair behavior toward the Taiwanese, the *tangwei* did not support Taiwan's independence movement, but wanted political power." Part of the opposition's power rested with the native Taiwanese "*bensheng ren*" who viewed themselves as marginalized by the Mainlander "*waisheng ren*" minority.[27]

In December 1979, a peaceful protest of opposition party supporters and free press advocates for the magazine Formosa turned violent. The southern city of Kaohsiung, long a hotbed of the opposition "tangwei," saw serious disturbances and subsequent arrests. The Kaohsiung Incident was a very clear warning to the central government that an increasingly educated, and a spring middle class population, would no longer settle for the politics as usual of the undisputed KMT.

In September 1986, a new political party calling itself the Democratic Progressive Party (DPP) illegally formed. The DPP charter did not advocate creation of an independent Taiwan. The KMT government nonetheless did not crack down. Yet, according to Dr. Myers, "But in 1989, some DPP leaders, declared their support for a higher goal than Taiwan's democratization: to establish a Republic of Taiwan with a new constitution affirming Taiwan's separation from Mainland China." In October 1991, the DPP charter was amended, "The residents of Taiwan will decide their destiny, and the Taiwan people will vote on whether to establish a Republic of Taiwan and redraft the Constitution."[28]

Despite its democratic intent, the DPP directly challenged both the domestic and international situation for Taiwan. Though in opposition to the ruling KMT, the DPP was now directly challenging the core principle of both the ROC and PRC states for that matter; namely, that Taiwan was "China."

With the election of Ronald Reagan as US President, the style if not substance of relations with Taiwan changed. Long a supporter of the ROC while still the Governor of California, President Reagan was an unquestionable supporter of Taiwan. Reagan moreover had severe misgivings about the entire relationship with the People's Republic.

Yet, despite some will of the wisp fanciful thinking that the conservative President would switch back diplomatic ties to Taipei, there was nothing of the sort.

Alexander Haig, Reagan's Secretary of State "had made a name for himself as an outspoken 'China supporter.' He used the phrase 'strategic imperative' to describe China," James Lilley recounts adding, "Haig wanted to give China a preferential status in the formulation of U.S. foreign policy because, like Kissinger, he saw it as a valuable counterweight to the Soviet Union. ... Haig was intent on pushing through his vision of a partnership with China."[29]

Fox Butterfield, the *New York Times* Peking Bureau Chief, wrote,

"Taiwan poses a delicate continuing problem for President Reagan, particularly the issue of U.S. arms sales to the Nationalists. The Communists were annoyed by Reagan's pro-Taiwan rhetoric during the presidential campaign. ... Peking was outraged by the Reagan Administration's decision in January 1982 to allow Taiwan to buy more F-5E jet fighters, claiming it constituted interference in China internal affairs, even though the Nationalists were disappointed that Washington turned down their request for a new, more advanced aircraft."[30]

The matter of continuing American arms sales to Taiwan became an issue in 1982. While the PRC pushed for a cessation in the US for selling defensive weapons to Taiwan, the USA was looking for a balanced approach. After eight months of contentious negotiations, the PRC and USA came to an agreement on 17 August, whereby both sides issued a joint communiqué. Washington agreed to "gradually reduce its sales of arms to Taiwan, leading over a period of time, to a final resolution." Not surprisingly, the text did not give any specific timeframe nor specifics on which weapons platforms to cancel. Nonetheless, while lacking specifics, the document signaled a long-term policy intent.[31]

Despite a joint communiqué being a statement of intended policy, this document was neither an Executive Agreement nor a Treaty and did not entail specific legal obligations. The document nonetheless could significantly hinder Taiwan's defensive force modernization.

Earlier in the year, James Lilley had taken up his new post as Director of the AIT, the Washington's very unofficial but still de facto outpost on Taiwan. Given that the USA has established *de jure* diplomatic ties with the PRC, the AIT, despite it being deliberately under the radar status, had the amazingly important de facto role in representing America's huge commercial relations and cultural ties with Taiwan.

Just before the August communiqué, Lilly met with President Chiang Ching-kuo to offer the assurances that "they would not be abandoned by the Reagan Administration. They reaffirmed that the U.S. would live up to the guidelines of the Taiwan Relations Act by not setting a specific date by which arms sales to Taiwan would end and by not pressuring Taiwan to negotiate with Peking." Director Lilly added, "The assurances cushioned the anxiety and uneasiness of the Taiwan leadership over the August Communique and were, I think, a direct contrast to the shoddy way in which Taiwan had been handled during normalization with Communist China ... for Reagan, maintaining the balance of power across the Taiwan Strait had to be the departure point for U.S. foreign policy."[32]

Cousin Lee's Confidence

That balance between the governments on both sides of the Taiwan Strait brought Taiwan a new breathing space and some could argue a new confidence. With the quiet assurances from the Reagan Administration, gone were the looming shadows from China, at least for the time being. Taiwan in the 1980s became a vibrant place, thriving socially and prospering economically. A confident middle class was becoming a pillar of an accepted political reality; that Taiwan was their home and the Mainland was another place. Landing in Taipei for the first time in 1975, I can still vividly recall signs when leaving the Sungshan airport to "Recover the Mainland." On a trip in the early 1980s, the same signs in the plaza were replaced by ads for trade shows and electronics companies.

The popular songs of Teresa Teng (Tung Li-yun) became a soundtrack for this decade on Taiwan and very importantly on the Mainland too where, despite the taboo, people clandestinely listened to the often soulful and melancholy ballads which wafted across the Taiwan Strait.

Taiwan was gaining self-confidence, and the Chiang Ching-kuo era was well summarized by a drawing by the Israeli-American cartoonist Raanan Lurie showing a young, fit, and confident martial arts player with the ROC flag proudly on his tunic. "Cousin Lee," as the image was called, was commissioned by the Taiwan government to promote the island's image in the 1980s. In many ways an Israeli cartoonist could understand Taiwan; the shopworn David and Goliath image was as alive between tiny Taiwan and the Mainland as it was between Israel and the Arabs. The Israel analogy was a perfect metaphor for Taiwan in many ways; a small, spunky, and resilient land especially during the 1970s and 1980s.

As with Israel, Taiwan's military was lean, mean, and tough; its Air Force though hopelessly outnumbered had good aircraft but better pilots and maintenance. In 1979, Taiwan military stood at 539,000 for all services but equally backed by huge reserves. Defense expenditure stood at $1.7 billion. Though the PRC military weighed in at 4.3 million and estimates for military spending were $46 billion, yet in 1979, much of the PRC inventory was outdated and in poor maintenance, especially in the Air Force.[33]

Naturally, modernization has been a Taiwan hallmark. As the island shifted from agriculture and labor-intensive industries, the electronics and computer industries came to the fore. The Hsinchu Science-based industrial park was founded in 1980 as Taiwan's answer to Silicon Valley. The National Science Council established Hsinchu park to serve as a nexus for innovative research and development. Computer makers, biotechnology firms, and telecommunications companies quickly made Hsinchu both a research and a production center. In 1992, the park sold over three billion dollars' worth of technology products. This would be just the beginning.³⁴

Economically, Taiwan's factories and computer were humming in the late 1980s too. Economic growth reached a dizzying 12 percent in 1986 and 1987, and only cooled down to 6 percent by 1992. Wages kept pace with per capita incomes. The per capita GNP jumped from $4000 in 1986 to $8000 in 1990 to $10,215 in 1992. Foreign trade reached $153 billion in 1992, the USA remained the major market with 29 percent of trade. Yet, trade with Hong Kong, which was often transshipment trade to Mainland China, was surging quickly and had become Taiwan's second largest market.³⁵

Despite its proximity and cultural ties, trade with Mainland China was basically illegal before 1979. Given that both Peking and Taipei were still political adversaries, what trade took place was carried out via the third-party intermediary of Hong Kong, which still reminded British Crown Colony. Indirect trade with the Mainland reached $466 million in 1981 from a paltry $76 million in 1979. This was only the beginning; in 1988, two-way trade reached $2.2 billion, and by 1992, Taiwan's indirect trade with China jumped to $7.4 billion. Taiwan's exports to the Mainland flourished and, in 1992, the island had a hefty trade surplus of $5 billion for the year.³⁶

Hidden in those figures was a growing trade and equally investment dependence on China. Significant trade surpluses which favored Taipei, nonetheless, made Taiwan more dependent on China, who through its massively large trade surpluses with the USA, could easily underwrite this unfavorable relationship with its wayward cousins on Taiwan.

During this period, Taiwan excelled in what I call diplomacy by trade; despite not having formal diplomatic ties with the USA, Canada, or the European countries, the island has thriving commercial ties represented by local de facto trade offices and consulates in Taipei. Beyond the AIT, in 1986, Canada established a very unofficial Canadian Trade Office to oversee booming commerce. In 1986, two-way trade stood at nearly $2 billion, by 1991, it had reached 2.6 billion. Germany is Taiwan's largest European trade partner; since 1972, when diplomatic links were severed, trade went from $227 million to $7.5 billion in 1992. Taipei hosts over 40 informal trade offices including the German Institute Taipei, the Malaysian Friendship/Trade Center, Manila Economic and Cultural Office, and the Singapore Trade Office. Likewise, 15 American states maintain trade legations in Taipei.³⁷

> *Trilateral US Trade with ROC versus PRC* The USA was long Taiwan's number 1 trading partner. Even a full decade after Washington opened diplomatic ties with Beijing in 1979, the USA trade with Taiwan exceeded the trade with the PRC. The balance shifted after 1993. USA–Taiwan trade that year was $41 billion. USA–PRC trade was close behind at $40 billion. Indeed, by 1994, the balance tipped where America's commerce with Taiwan was $44 billion but trade with China edged up to $48 billion; with a $29 billion deficit for the USA. A decade later in 2004, US trade with Taiwan reached $56 billion while PRC commerce surged to $231 billion, now with a $162 billion deficit favoring Beijing. By 2014, US's two-way trade with China hit a high of $590 billion with a deficit of $343 billion. American trade with Taiwan in the same period stood at $67 billion with the USA facing a $14 billion deficit.
> *Source*: US Trade by Country **census.gov/foreign-trade**

President Chiang was playing a good defensive game if warily watching his political flanks from both across the Taiwan Strait and domestically among an increasingly empowered domestic opposition. Chiang had confided in Reagan Administration officials his plans for political reform on Taiwan. Basically, the ROC president was following a four-point plan: democratization, beginning a process of Taiwanization of the government, maintain prosperity, and opening up to China.[38]

The KMT government took the first nervous steps to wider democratization. The political climate became freer but not free in the early 1980s. Lee Teng-hui, a native Taiwanese educated in Japan and also with a Ph.D. from Cornell University, had been Governor of Taiwan Province. Lee was elected Vice President in 1984. On the sudden death of Chiang Ching-guo in January 1988, Lee filled out the remainder of the late president term. In March 1990, Lee Teng-hui was elected by the National Assembly to serve as ROC president. He was 67 years old.[39]

The Taiwanese had become well educated and increasingly involved as being successful entrepreneurs and thus supporting the economic miracle. The Chiang government would try to entice many of these Taiwanese, especially the technocrats, into the administration. As Ted Galen Carpenter writes,

"In this formulation the 'hard' authoritarianism that Chiang had inherited from his father constituted essentially a dictatorship that used mainlander control of the KMT and elections as ways to consolidate power of the leader. Under the new 'soft' authoritarianism, indigenous Taiwanese would be co-opted into the KMT, and although the government would remain securely under KMT rule, elections would allow for incremental responses to social change and other pressures that were growing among the governed."[40]

There was one major legacy of Chiang Ching-kuo's era which is largely now forgotten: the lifting of "The Emergency Decree in the Taiwan Area." The Legislative Assembly unanimously lifted martial law, in July 1987. Largely a legacy of the 1950s, the law was nonetheless used indiscriminately as a pretext to control dissent and opposition.

In May 1991, the ROC President Lee Teng-hui formally ended the civil war with China, with the termination of the "Period of National Mobilization for Suppression of the Communist Rebellion." Taipei's fundamental policies toward Beijing can be summed up as "one China, two political entities" "The ROC's use of the term 'entity' instead of 'state' or 'government' is a pragmatic characterization of the political reality acorns the Taiwan Strait, allowing sufficient 'creative ambiguity' for each side to live with."[41]

Importantly, what became known as the 1992 Consensus has served as a practical framework for relations on both sides of the Taiwan Strait. In late 1992, unofficial delegations of both Beijing's Association for Relations Across the Taiwan Strait (ARATS) and Taipei's "Straits Exchange Foundation (SEF)" met in Hong Kong. A tacit understanding was verbally reached in what became later labeled the "1992 Consensus." Both sides recognized that there is one China, but each side can have its own interpretation of what China stands for. For Beijing, China is the People's Republic of China. For Taipei, China remains the Republic of China. The term "1992 Consensus" actually dates from 2000 when a ranking KMT official Su Chi coined the phrase. The Consensus has served as a *modus vivendi* for relations but was widely criticized by Taiwan's opposition parties ever since.[42]

For the first 40 years, Taiwan clearly held the socio-economic high ground vis-à-vis Mainland China. Yet, despite Taiwan's impressive economic clout, Deng Xiaoping's amazing economic reforms on the Mainland, started in 1978, were now in full bloom.

The Chinese economy was beginning to matter; Chinese politics were not globally confrontational (except to Taiwan) and the once reviled People's Republic of China was now largely accepted into polite company. Despite the communist crackdown on pro-democracy students in Tiananmen

Square in June 1989, and the temporary international revulsion toward the PRC, political rationalization soon triumphed, and by the early 1990s the PRC was again accepted if more warily.

Nonetheless, despite Taiwan's stunning impressive socio/economic statistics, there was a far more subtle political sea change taking place on the small island. This was the transformative effect of economics on the political democratization process itself. There is often a direct correlation between economic improvement and growing social expectations prying upon often closed political doors. This was clearly the case in Taiwan, where in fact, the democratic process was not marked by the same fitful bumps and civil violence induced change as in either South Korea or the Philippines.

In the *Foreign Affairs* essay "How Development Leads to Democracy," authors Ronald Inglehart and Christian Welzel state,

> "modernization is a syndrome of social changes linked to industrialization. Once set in motion, it tends to penetrate all aspects of life, bringing occupational specialization, urbanization, rising educational levels, rising life expectancy, and rapid economic growth. These create a self-enforcing process that transforms social life and political institutions, bringing mad participation in politics, and in the long run, making the establishment of democratic political institutions increasingly likely."[43]

Taiwan entered the 1990s with a vibrant economy and a democratizing political system. Though the Taipei government was faced with diplomatic isolation, Taiwan's diplomacy by trade made the ROC a still formidable, if often overlooked, player. For Taiwan, the 1990s became a decade of political confidence and economic sophistication where the island made its proud debut on the global stage.

Notes

1. Thomas J. Bellows. Taiwan's Foreign Policy in the 1970s: A Case Study in Adaptation and Viability, Occasional Papers/Reprints Series in Contemporary Asian Studies Number 4, School of Law. University of Maryland, 1977, p. 6.
2. FRUS, China 1969–1972, Vol. XVII, (Washington, DC: U.S. Government Printing Office, 2006), p. 815.
3. Henry Kissinger. *Diplomacy*. (New York: Simon & Schuster, 1994), pp. 727–728.
4. Ibid. p. 729.

5. Michael Yahuda. *The International Politics of the Asia-Pacific, 1945–1995.* (London: Rutledge, 1997), p. 134.
6. China Yearbook 1972–1973, pp. 143–144.
7. Ibid. pp. 156–158.
8. Ibid. pp. 160–162.
9. Ibid. pp. 173–183.
10. Sun Yat-sen. *San Min Chu I/The Three Principles of the People.* (Chungking: Ministry of Information of the Republic of China, 1943).
11. China Yearbook 1972, p. 246.
12. Shirley W.Y. Kuo, Gustav Ranis, John C.H. Fei. The Taiwan Success Story: Rapid Growth with Improved Distribution in the Republic of China 1952–1979. (Boulder, CO: Westview Press, 1981), p. 11.
13. Ibid. pp. 23–24.
14. Ibid. pp. 25–26.
15. Op. cit. China Yearbook 1972–1973, p. 252.
16. Ibid. pp. 254–255.
17. Economic Development in the Republic of China. (Taipei: Ministry of Economic Affairs, 1975), p. 8.
18. Ten Major Construction Projects, (Taipei: China Publishing, 1974), pp. 2–6.
19. Taiwan's Foreign Policy in the 1970s, p. 8.
20. President Chiang Kai-shek; His Life Story in Pictures, (Taipei, Government Information Office, 1972), p. 171.
21. "ROC Bids Farewell to President," Free China Weekly, Taipei, Taiwan 20 April 1975, p. 1.
22. Op. cit. International Politics of the Asia-Pacific, p. 137.
23. James Lilley. China Hands: Nine Decades of Adventure, Espionage, and Diplomacy in Asia. (New York: Public Affairs, 2004), p. 209.
24. Ibid. pp. 211–212.
25. FRUS, 1977–1980. China Volume XIII, (Washington, DC: Government Printing Office, 2013), pp. 659–660.
26. Qimao Chen, "New Approaches in China's Foreign Policy." Asian Survey 27 (November 1987), pp. 117–1171 and PRC Press/UN 30 September 1981.
27. Myers, Ramon H. and Jialin Zhang. *The Struggle Across the Taiwan Strait; The Divided China Problem.* Stanford, CA: Hoover Institution Press, 2006, pp. 48–49.
28. Ibid. pp. 50–51.

29. Op. cit. "New Approaches in China's Foreign Policy," pp. 228–229. General Alexander Haig, having served as the military commander of NATO was well aware of the growing Soviet military buildup and was thus, along with many West Europeans, enchanted with playing the "China Card" against Moscow.
30. Fox Butterfield. *China: Alive in the Bitter Sea*. (New York: Times Books, 1982), p. 453.
31. U.S. Department of State: Office of the Historian 17 August 1982 and PRC/Press United Nations, August 1982, p. 1.
32. Op. cit. China Hands, pp. 247–248.
33. The Military Balance 1979–1980. (London: International Institute for Strategic Studies, 1979), pp. 60–61, 64–65, 95.
34. The Republic of China Yearbook 1994. (Taipei: Government Information Office, 1993), p. 335.
35. Ibid. pp. 198–200.
36. Ibid. p. 201.
37. Financial Post, 26 October 1987 and John J. Metzler, *Divided Dynamism The Diplomacy of Separated Nations: Germany, Korea, China*/second edition (Lanham, MD: University Press of America, 2014), pp. 175–176.
38. Op. cit. China Hands, p. 257.
39. Op. cit. ROC Yearbook 1994, p. XV.
40. Ted Galen Carpenter. *America's Coming War With China; A Collision Course Over Taiwan*. (New York: Palgrave Macmillan, 2005), p. 60.
41. The Republic of China Yearbook 1995. (Taipei: Government Information Office, 1995), p. 143.
42. "1992 Consensus Between Beijing and Taipei Appears Here to Stay," South China Morning Post 14 December 2012, SCMP.com
43. "How Development Leads to Democracy—What We Know About Modernization," by Ronald Inglehart and Christian Welzel. Foreign Affairs, March/April 2009.

CHAPTER 5

The Republic of China on Taiwan 1993–1999

The 1990s emerged as an optimistic time for Taiwan. The economy was humming along nicely, lifestyles were visibly improving, and the political process was showing a surprising democratic rejuvenation. Indeed, the early years of Lee Teng-hui's presidency and the noticeable *Taiwanization* process throughout the government were making the island a more socially equitable place. In so many ways, social modernity and democratization were challenging the Confucian values the government was so fond of officially embracing.

By the early 1990s, there were over 50 political parties, of which 3 remained major players.

The long-ruling KMT nationalist party remained strong but not monolithic; in fact, while the KMT remained wedded to the one-China policy, at the same time, it had become the agent of change with the fast promotion of long-overlooked *Taiwanization* policies. Thus, while the KMT in Taiwan's early years was indisputably rooted in the "Mainlander" minority community on the island, during the 1990s the party was modernizing, realizing that the "Taiwanese majority" was also part of the national *tableaux*.

The DPP formed the principal opposition party. The DPP was rooted strongly in the Taiwanese opposition politics and identified with a Taiwanese rather than a Chinese identity. In October 1991, the DPP advocated *de jure* independence for Taiwan which directly confronts the KMT's "one-China" policy and, moreover, would trigger serious concern from Mainland China. The party which has many factions, nonetheless, is rooted in the Taiwanese experience.

The New Party was set up in 1993 as a movement to attract disenchanted KMT voters who were dissatisfied with both the ruling party's performance and practices and the DPP's increasingly radical stands on Taiwan independence.

Legislative elections in late 1992 produced a stunning result for the newly formed DPP. While the KMT gained 53 percent of the votes and 102 seats in the legislature, the DPP garnered 31 percent and 51 seats. Other parties won 16 percent. The elections illustrated what was emerging as a healthy opposition political scene. The opposition would score bigger wins in 1993 in elections for Municipal mayors and county magistrates, where in the popular vote the KMT won 48 percent and the DPP gained 41 percent, along with the New Party's 3 percent.[1]

By 1993, economic growth reached 5.87 percent, while Taiwan's trade with the rest of the world grew to $162 billion. Interestingly, Mainland trade grew to $15 billion, of which $14 billion represented Taiwan exports to the Mainland. At the same time, Taiwan firms had invested $3.6 billion in China, though the numbers were actually much higher.[2]

Cross–Strait "Coexistence"

Lee Teng-hui, in his first State of the Nation address in 1993 implored, "Taiwan and the Mainland are integral parts of China, and all Chinese have blood links." He added that Beijing should consider the future of all Chinese and "enhance two-way exchanges to narrow the difference in ideas and systems."[3]

Economic interactions between both sides of the Taiwan Strait brought about unofficial institutions to monitor and regulate the commerce. In 1991, the Taipei government established a cabinet-level Mainland Affairs Council (MAC) as a policy planner for unofficial contact with the PRC. That same year, Taipei set up the semi-official Straits Exchange Foundation (SEF) to deal with the Mainland in civil disputes and commercial matters. Beijing correspondingly established the ARATS. It was through such cooperative efforts that the historic "1992 Consensus" was created, whereby both governments agreed there is but one China but subject to each other's interpretation.

The government-funded SEF was created as a private body to circumvent the official policy of no official contact with the PRC. The SEF tends to be business-oriented and seeking contacts with the Mainland, whereas the MAC, being an official policy maker, takes a more cautious approach. In 1993, the SEF and ARATS hosted high-level talks in Singapore which were focused on opening effective communication channels, protection of rights and benefits of Taiwan businessmen in Mainland China, and safeguards for freedom and property. The SEF Chairman C.F. Koo stressed, "From now on Chinese on both sides of the Straits should renounce the zero-sum logic and champion the win-win concept instead." Both SEF and the ARATS remain unofficial mechanisms for managing relations, not solving intractable political issues.[4]

> *The 1992 Consensus* The "consensus" is an informal agreement between both the ROC and PRC to agree there is but *one China* but with different interpretations. In other words, both sides of the Taiwan Strait recognize the existence of one China but agree to differ on its specific definition. The consensus is really a *modus vivendi* reached by the MAC's former Chairman Su Chi to allow for both flexibility and ambiguity.
> Though the term "1992 Consensus" has emerged as a cornerstone for the KMT but as a punching bag for the opposition, the fact remains that the consensus allows for flexibility rather than political rigidity in ties between Taipei and Beijing. Importantly, the "consensus" offers both sides political common ground.
> *Source*: "1992 Consensus Verified by History: Ma," China Post 15 May 2015, p. 1

Correspondingly, in the early 1990s, Taiwan was feeling both more self-assertive and secure on both the political and economic fronts. After all, the small island was clearly a commercial power and economic force despite its diplomatic isolation. Quite normally, many Taiwanese were quite perplexed on how they were not seen or noticed on the international front. Thus, an emboldened DPP felt that a campaign to rejoin the UN would be a logical if not overdue step.

The DPP opposition pushed the UN issue back on a wary KMT government agenda. The move was logical but, at the same time, flawed. By 1993, three forces coalesced which encouraged Taiwan to regain the UN seat. First, with the UN representing universality, and given the large increase in new member states with the collapse of the former Soviet Union and subsequently Yugoslavia, the timing seemed perfect. Second, in 1991, both South and North Korea, long blocked by a cold war logjam, joined the UN as two separate states representing the Korean nation. Third, political pressures in Taiwan's rapidly changing democratic landscape saw political pressures pushing for a bigger international role and personality for Taiwan.

Moreover, in the anxious aftermath of the Tiananmen Square crackdown by the Chinese communists, most political pundits felt that this was a perfect time for Taiwan to try to reenter the UN. If it were not for the fact that the Beijing government held not only the China seat but more significantly a position on the Security Council with veto powers, this may have been possible. Thus, given the PRC's position of being "the sole legitimate government of China," and almost theological policy against a "two China" policy, the UN membership move would prove near impossible.

ROC Foreign Minister Frederick Chien, in a landmark article in *Foreign Affairs*, spoke of "pragmatic diplomacy" aimed at the island's survival. He stated, "pragmatic diplomacy is part and parcel to the ROC's democratic transformation ... just as Taiwan is part of China, so is the Mainland. Both should recognize that two different systems exist in these separate parts of China."[5]

United Nations Redux?

Nevertheless, in August 1993, seven of Taipei's allies in Central America submitted a letter to the Secretary General Boutros Boutros Ghali requesting "consideration" of the ROC–Taiwan membership in the General Assembly. The bid fizzled in the committee. The following year, 15 states unsuccessfully petitioned that Taiwan's status be discussed. During the 1994 Assembly session, 20 speakers, among them Nicaragua's Violetta Chamorro, called for ROC readmission. Indeed, the ROC government meets all the classical criteria for recognition under the Montevideo Convention and moreover Taiwan's population exceeds that of 140 UN members; its GNP is higher than all of 18 of the then 185 members.[6]

The UN debate triggered a political typhoon on both sides of the Taiwan Strait. Part of Taiwan's position was that in 1973, despite political division, both German governments (FRG and GDR) gained separate seats in the UN and held them until reunification in 1990. Equally, after years of complex political maneuvers, both separate Korean states (ROK and DPRK) gained UN membership in 1991 and still hold their separate seats. In both cases, the applications had to pass through the Security Council, where the PRC's Great Wall clearly blocks Taiwan's membership.

For example in 1995, 20 of Taipei's allies petitioned that Taiwan's "participation" be included as an Agenda item: "Consideration of the exceptional situation of the Republic of China on Taiwan in the international context, based on the principle of universality and in accordance with the established model of parallel representation of divided countries in the United Nations." Though the complex bid was killed in the committee, over 20 Foreign Ministers supported Taipei's position.

PRC Foreign Minister Qian Qichen warned delegates, "There is but one China in the world. The Government of the People's Republic of China is the sole legal government of China. It is the sole representative of China in the United Nations. And Taiwan is an indisputable part of China."[7]

Each year since a group of Taiwan's allies have proposed an agenda item to at least "discuss" varied and sundry options and formulae for Taiwan to participate in the UN General Assembly. Each session, at least 15 Foreign Ministers mention the issue from the marble rostrum of the Assembly. In 1998, 11 of Taipei's diplomatic allies requested the "participation of the Republic of China in the United Nations should be included in the agenda of the fifty-third regular session of the General Assembly." The exact wording of the proposed Agenda item was "The need to review General Assembly resolution 2758 (XXVI) of 25 October 1971 owing to the fundamental change in the international situation and to the coexistence of two Governments across the Taiwan Strait."[8] This attempt to schedule an agenda item would specifically challenge the 1971 resolution which expelled the "representatives of Chiang Kai-shek from the place which they unlawfully occupy at the United Nations."

This attempt was immediately rebuffed by Beijing Ambassador Qin Huasun, who called the move "a brazen attempt to challenge General Assembly resolution 2758 (XXVI), create 'two Chinas' or 'one China, one Taiwan' in the United Nations and split a sovereign state."[9]

Though the UN bid failed to gain international traction, on the domestic front, impressive economic and now indeed socio-political changes swept this era. A hopeful wave of change and fractious, if genuine, democratization now swept Taiwan. Fiercely contested presidential elections in 1996 saw Lee Teng-hui, a native Taiwanese (educated in Japan moreover) of the Nationalist Party, Chiang Kai-shek's old if now re-branded KMT. At the same time, the democratization process was challenged, or should we say haunted, by the old taboos of post-war Taiwan society. It was more openly threatened by Beijing's rhetorical and military saber rattling to intimidate voters.

1996 Presidential Election

President Lee was a native Hokkien-speaking Taiwanese, not a Mainland Mandarin. Equally, he was one of the many technocrats the KMT had groomed for governance. As Governor of Taiwan province, Lee made a name for himself in the rarefied rural regions where the Taiwanese identity was the strongest. One could say Lee was a popular technocrat.

As Prof. Shelley Rigger recounts,

> "The early 1990s saw a cascade of democratic 'firsts': the first election the all-new National Assembly members in 1991, the first election of an all-new Legislative Yuan in 1992, the reintroduction of directly elected Kaohsiung city and Taipei City mayors in 1994, the first direct election of the provincial governor in 1994, and in 1996, the first popular presidential election, which made Lee Teng-hui the first person in history to be directly elected to lead an ethnic Chinese nation."[10]

The extraordinary 1996 elections were carried out against the backdrop and bluster of Beijing's "missile diplomacy," which shadowed the political contest. Taiwan's presidential election brought the Chinese dragons to the point of dueling. By pressing ahead with free and fair elections, Taiwan was quite frankly embarrassing the PRC as well as giving the Marxist Mandarins the impression that the island may grab formal independence. Beijing launched a round of crude saber rattling toward Taiwan and added some missile shots into the nearby waters.

As the elections approached, the PRC fired off a salvo of M-11 intermediate range missiles into the waters of Keelung and Kaohsiung ports so as to disrupt shipping and reinforce the island's sense of vulnerability. But Beijing's message was a blunt as it was counterproductive. The Clinton

Administration subsequently sent two aircraft carrier battle groups, the Independence and the Nimitz, to Taiwan waters, thus sending an unmistakable signal that Washington is warily watching. PRC Premier Li Peng protested but refrained from further saber rattling. From an American viewpoint, the dispatch of two carrier battle groups to Taiwan evoked the era of the 1950s not the mid-1990s. From the viewpoint of anxious and invigorated Taiwan voters, the island would rally round the flag.

"The results of the Taiwan Strait Crisis were ambiguous. China lost ground diplomatically. But it did convey the message that it would respond if Taiwan made moves that displeased it. China also left open the possibility that there will be further tests of wills with the United States in the Western Pacific, especially as China's Navy becomes a bigger and more credible force," advised Bernstein and Munro.[11]

Yet, the crux of the matter was less about Beijing's perceptions of Lee than the PRC's long-term fear over widening democratization on a Chinese-speaking island just 80 miles off the Mainland. "At the time that China embarked on its March 1996 exercise in intimidation, a few pundits identified the real issue as not so much Taiwanese independence but Taiwanese democracy. Genuine popular sovereignty on Taiwan threatened to undermine the authority of the dictatorship in Beijing," added the authors in *The Coming Conflict with China*.[12]

Elections went forward and Lee's KMT won again. With 76 percent of eligible voters turning out, Lee and his Vice President Lien Chan (Mainland born) received 54 percent of the vote, while the DPP's Peng Ming-min got 21 percent and the New Party obtained 15 percent. During the same March election, Taiwan voters were electing members to the Third National Assembly where the ruling KMT garnered 50 percent of the votes and 183 of the 334 contested seats. The DPP won 30 percent of the vote and gained 99 seats. The maverick New Party gained 15 percent of the vote and 46 seats.[13]

Yet, in Lee's second term, there was a clear and perceptible *Taiwanization* of many names, the political lexicon, and national identity.

One may ask: *Is Taiwan* Chinese, Taiwanese, or both? The fractious social and political debate on *National Identity*, Chinese-ness, had long been a thorn and taboo topic in the first 30 years of the ROC on Taiwan. Now who was "Chinese" mattered both socially and politically too.

The official story went something like this. Most of Taiwan's current inhabitants, the Taiwanese majority, had emigrated from coastal China (especially Fukien province) centuries earlier but had acclimatized to the tropical island. The small aborigine minority was viewed in purely folkloric terms. During the Japanese colonial period 1895–1945, many Taiwanese profited both economically, educationally as well as in the local political arena. After "Restoration" to the ROC in October 1945, and especially after the fall of the Nationalist government on the Mainland, a few million Chinese mostly military and civil servants came to Taiwan and viewed the island as a temporary refuge but springboard for Mainland recovery. By the 1990s, approximately 84 percent of the population were Taiwanese while 14 percent were Mainlander.

The official KMT view reflected "we are all Chinese" and for those Taiwanese who disagreed the opprobrium was either that "they had become good Japanese" (a dire insult) or if they became too involved in opposition politics, they would often be arrested. Thus, looking through the prism of Taiwan politics from, say, 1950 to 1980 one saw a successful Chinese island province, which combined Confucian values, hard work, and the nostalgia for one's home province on the Mainland. Realistically, the paradigm began to change as the older Mainlanders passed away and their children, while still wedded to the China nostalgia and the KMT, realized that Taiwan was their home but the Mainland could be their investment market and production base.

In the 1990s, activists used the term "Taiwan-centric consciousness," which basically reflected the view that the island should be viewed as having unique cultural and social characteristics, and not a footnote to wider Chinese narrative. According to Prof. Rigger, speaking "Taiwanese," which is really Hokkien, became a marker of belonging. Chauvinism on the part of the newly emboldened Taiwanese began to outshine the Mainlanders. Rigger states that the children of the Mainlanders, although born on Taiwan, began to feel as second-class citizens. President Lee Teng-hui (Japanese and Hokkien speaking) began to mend the rift among the island's ethnic groups. He used a phrase "New Taiwanese" to redefine Mainlanders as belonging to and in Taiwan. "New Taiwanese," according to Lee, comprised all the people on the island irrespective of their provincial heritage or linguistic dialect.[14]

At the beginning of the Lee Teng-hui era (and recall Lee was a product of Japanese Imperial education), there were a number of clear and unambiguous statements that Taiwan is NOT pushing for *de jure* "independence" despite, for all practical purposes, having de facto independence on the island since 1949.

Yet, the opposition DPP defined itself in a Taiwanese mold going so far as to press for Taiwan independence, a political lightning rod to the

Beijing communist regime. Indeed, the PRC has never renounced the use of force to "take back" Taiwan to the motherland, and this proves the ultimate excuse.

For the ROC government, defending its embryonic democracy and prosperous lifestyle depended on a strong but nimble military force. In 1996, at the time of the elections and saber rattling from across the Straits, Taiwan's total armed forces stood at 376,000 with defense spending of $13.6 billion. Military spending comprised 4.9 percent of GDP. In contrast, China's military stood at 2.9 million with spending reflecting 5.7 percent of GDP. By this time, however, the PRC's huge but technically moribund military was being significantly rejuvenated with modern weapons programs.[15]

Just two years after the US Navy deployments to the Taiwan Strait, a Department of Defense

> "East Asian Strategy Report 1998" stated, "The United States maintains robust but unofficial relations with the people on Taiwan, government by the Taiwan Relations Act (TRA) and guided by three U.S.-PRC joint communiqués ... the United States sells defensive arms to Taiwan to enable it to maintain a sufficient self-defense capability. Our limited arms sales have contributed to maintaining peace and stability in the Taiwan Strait and to creating an atmosphere conductive to the improvement of cross-Strait relations, including dialogue."[16]

Hong Kong Rumblings

The 1997 Hong Kong handover proved an anxious time for Taiwan. Indeed, the countdown for the transfer of the British Crown Colony to Chinese sovereignty was outlined a decade earlier in a deal between Deng Xiaoping and Prime Minister Margaret Thatcher. The outlines of the agreement were clear and allowed for Hong Kong's inhabitants to have guaranteed rights and freedoms for a 50-year period. Yet, the reversion of this prosperous and vibrant city state into a "Special Administrative Region" (SAR) of the People's Republic of China created a practical example of Deng's suggested "one Country, Two Systems" formula for Taiwan. And, given that Beijing's mandarins would not kill Hong Kong's "golden goose which laid the golden eggs," the image of a prosperous and relatively free SAR troubled Taiwan.

Having been in Hong Kong and Taiwan immediately after the handover, the images wafted across the region like the drifting smoke from the spectacular fireworks display on Victoria Peak. The smell of change was in the air. There was a quiet nervousness. Would Beijing behave?

Jiang Zemin, President of the PRC, proclaimed triumphantly on the first day of Beijing's rule over Hong Kong, "The prospect of complete unification is now in sight; the 'one country, two systems' formula for Hong Kong and Macao would set an example for the final solution to the Taiwan question." Days later at a press conference in Taipei, a nervously confident Lien Chan, Premier of the ROC on Taiwan, retorted that Hong Kong was after all a colony whereas the ROC remains a sovereign state and democratic country. Speaking as afternoon skies darkened and storm clouds rumbled, Premier Lien stated, "The ROC's situation is different from Hong Kong. China has been ruled as two separate political entities for almost 50 years. Unification must be accomplished on the basis of freedom and democracy." Lien added, "We cannot consider the democratic rights of our people as bargaining chip which can be given away to appease an unelected and unrepresentative government in Beijing."[17]

Yet, the emotional appeal of the former British colony being returned to "the Chinese motherland" was not limited to the Mainland. Despite the political undertones, some Mainlander friends of mine in Taipei whose families were true-blue KMT, nonetheless, viewed the "retrocession" of a former colony to China as a positive insofar as it ended another chapter in colonialism for the Chinese people. Thus, viewed through the prism of Chinese nationalism, the Hong Kong handover had a level of nuance many Westerners missed.

Though the political world was watching events as Britain's Union Flag was lowered for the last time in Hong Kong, elsewhere in Asia the first jolts of what would become the Asian Economic Crisis were rumbling throughout Southeast Asia. Despite the regional financial crisis, Taiwan GDP grew 6.8 percent in 1997 while per capita GNP reached an impressive $13,198. Taiwan now had achieved a GNP making the island the 20th largest economy in the world. Foreign trade that same year reached $236 billion, with the USA, Hong Kong (and the third-party indirect trade to the Mainland), and Japan being the principal partners. According to the ROC's official MAC, bilateral trade with the Mainland reached $24 billion in 1997. The balance of trade was overwhelmingly in Taiwan's favor, and even in this period, trade with the PRC amounted to 10 percent of all Taiwan's trade.[18]

Taiwan–Mainland Trade and Investment Soars Despite Political Void
Evoking Adam Smith's "invisible hand" guiding economic interests, Taiwan businessmen sought trade, investment, and markets on the Mainland despite the paucity of official links. In 1987, the ROC government legalized commerce with China. By 1994, two-way trade between Taiwan and China reached $16.5 billion, a sum representing about 9 percent of Taiwan's total trade. By 1999, trade reached $26 billion; and by 2000, $32 billion. As importantly, Taiwan's investment in Mainland China grew rapidly from $2 billion in 1990 and $3.4 billion the following year representing over 3800 projects. By 1992, Taiwan businessmen had invested up to $9 billion in over 10,000 projects. Most investments were in coastal China in Fukien and Guandong provinces. Investment was soon focused in the high-tech and computer industries. Since 2005, China has become Taiwan's number one trade partner.
Source: Bureau of Foreign Trade/Ministry of Economic Affairs, Taipei/Taiwan and Ricky Tung, "Economic Integration between Taiwan and South China's Fukien and Kwantung Provinces," *Issues & Studies* 29 (July 1993), pp. 28–30.

Mainland/Taiwan Trade

Despite Taipei's nervousness concerning the PRC's political intentions, the Lee Teng-hui era, nonetheless, slipped into a comfortable commercial relationship with the Mainland. John Chang, Taipei's former Minister of Overseas Chinese Affairs, put the matter into context; the Taiwan Strait have seen three phases of confrontation since 1949; the first 1949–1959 military confrontation, the second 1959–1987, peaceful confrontation; the third 1987 to the present, a separation eased by growing family and commercial ties across the Straits.[19]

The Cross–Strait dialogue, which characterized the era, was based on the tacit understanding of "one China." Following the 1992 Consensus, the arrangement was honed by the additional nuance. The SEF describes it as the "One China principle but subject to each other's interpretation." This reflects a shared view that there is only one China and they do not belong to separate states. According to Prof. Weishing Hu, "This is believed to be the cornerstone for cross-Straits relations." "On 9 July 1999, however,

Lee Teng-hui dropped a political bombshell in the Taiwan Strait. In an interview with Voice of Germany reporters, Lee openly challenged the One China principle and described cross-strait relations as 'state-to-state or at least special state-to-state relations (commonly referred to as the Two State theory)."[20]

Lee's remarks were considered highly provocative by the PRC. But, in the context of an interview with German reporters, the comments reflected the complex political dilemma of a divided nation which was de facto divided into two separate states. The ROC president may have been trying to illustrate the parallel with Germany's own experience in which two long-divided but separate state entities came to grudgingly recognize each other's existence in a landmark 1972 agreement.

Lee's role in actively shepherding Taiwan along the democratic path should not be underestimated. As Prof. Shelly Rigger states, "Lee Teng-hui was a prodigious force in Taiwan's modern history. He presided over the transformation of its domestic politics while deftly managing its fast-moving relations with the Mainland." She added, "He made it clear that whether Beijing's plan was to absorb Taiwan into the PRC or unite with the ROC in a marriage of equals, Taiwan would hold out for its own interests. He was wildly popular."[21]

Yet, with new presidential elections on the horizon in 2000, renewed political turbulence soon emerged between Taipei and Beijing.

Notes

1. *The Republic of China Yearbook 1995.* (Taipei: Government Information Office, 1995), pp. 133–134.
2. Ibid., pp. 205, 211.
3. China Post 5 January 1993.
4. John J. Metzler. Divided Dynamism: The Diplomacy of Separated Nations: Germany, Korea, China. (Lanham, MD: University Press of America, 2014), pp. 179–180 and Interview Dr. Chiang Pin-kung, SEF Taipei June 2011.
5. Chien, Frederick. "A View From Taipei," *Foreign Affairs* Winter 1991–92, pp. 93–103.
6. United Nations General Assembly A/48/191 9 August 1993, pp. 1–2 and *Washington Times* 20 December 1994.
7. PRC Press/UN 27 September 1995, pp. 7–8.
8. United Nations General Assembly A/53/145, July 1998.

9. United Nations General Assembly A/53/178, 13 July 1998, p. 1.
10. Shelley Rigger. Why Taiwan Matters Small Island, Global Powerhouse. (Lanham, MD: Rowman & Littlefield, 2011), p. 79.
11. Bernstein, Richard and Ross Munro. The Coming Conflict with China, pp. 155–156.
12. Ibid., p. 162.
13. The Republic of China Yearbook 1999, (Taipei: Government Information Office, 1999), pp. 111–112.
14. op. cit. Why Taiwan Matters, pp. 34–35.
15. Military Balance 1997/98. (London: International Institute for Strategic Studies, 1997), pp. 193, 295.
16. The United States Security Strategy for the East-Asia Pacific Region 1998. (Washington, DC: Department of Defense, 1998), pp. 34–35.
17. "The Future of Taiwan," Washington Times 11 August 1997, p. A17.
18. Op. cit. China Yearbook 1999, pp. 162–163, 167.
19. John Chang. "Current Political Developments in the ROC and Its Relations with Mainland China." Lecture/Center of Asian Studies St John's University, New York, 29 June 1993.
20. "Two State Theory" versus "One China Principle" Cross–Strait Relations in 1999. Weixing Hu. China Review. (Hong Kong: Chinese University Press, 2000), p. 135. pp. 135–156. Lee's remarks were made in a Deutsche Welle interview.
21. Op. cit. Why Taiwan Matters, p. 79.

CHAPTER 6

Taiwan (The Republic of China) 2000–2008

The election of the DPP proved a socio-political *tsunami* in Taiwan's landscape. Given that the vocally Taiwanese opposition party had been elected to the presidency, the island's entire political tone and tenor soon changed. Nonetheless, newly elected President Chen Shui-bian, a popular former Taipei major, won the race with a plurality 39 percent against a divided opposition. Former KMT stalwart James Soong, the popular Taiwan Governor, scored 37 percent while ironically the long-ruling KMT came in third with a lackluster performance by Lien Chan, the former Vice President who gained a 23 percent of the electorate.

Chen's narrow victory, despite its decisive ideological jolt to the *status quo*, still faced a legislature dominated by the KMT Nationalists.[1]

The DPP victory created a synthesis of mixed emotions, expectations, and exculpation. Emotions that the long-marginalized but dogged opposition party had won its first election on the national level, if only by a plurality. Expectations were naturally higher as the party stalwarts, initially restrained by Chen, would seek to transform the very nature of Taiwan, from the *status quo* Republic of China, to a newly energized and rebranded Taiwan. Exculpation would be a third factor; DPP had come through the political wilderness, was rooted in the struggle for Taiwanese identity, and comprise many members who had witnessed the harsh KMT crackdowns in the 1950s, the White Terror, which formed the crucible of opposition politics. Thus, on DPP and the shoulders of Chen Shui-bian rested the cusp of Taiwan's future.

DPP pressed for a transformative doctrine for Taiwan. Yet, much to the shock and chagrin of the still formidable KMT "pan Blue" bloc, the party would be fitful. Perhaps more importantly, the DPP's path was carefully monitored in both Beijing and Washington, albeit for different reasons.

For the PRC, Chen's statements and rhetoric would create a quiet fury which before long triggered serious and bellicose warnings over the outcome of Taiwan's presumed path to "separatism" or "independence." In direct inverse, the USA, long a close political and economic ally of Taiwan, felt that DPP's rhetoric over "separatism" could trigger a military confrontation with Beijing in which Washington would be pulled into militarily.

President Chen Shui-bian stressed the international personality of Taiwan as not being necessarily Chinese. Chen's many declarations, and spinning political weathervane of defining Taiwan, caused many sleepless nights in Beijing and indeed Washington. After all if Taiwan were to move from its accepted de facto independence and to attempt a more formal *de jure* statement of sovereignty, such a decision could provoke the PRC dragon to attack militarily. Such an attack could have wide East Asian strategic implications.

Many of Taiwan's successful entrepreneurs and businessmen, being native Taiwanese, naturally gravitated to the DPP. While the KMT was long rooted of the island *status quo* bureaucracy, civil service, military, and political elites, the DPP roughly represented "the other Taiwan" of small farmers, big businessmen, and mid-level entrepreneurs. The latter group was less wedded to the island's constantly refined versions of "Chineseness" than the business bottom line. The reality that Taiwan was really already an independent state was in the minds of many DPP stalwarts, not reflected in the rhetorically re-calibrated renditions of the Republic of China "on or in" Taiwan. Stated bluntly, many of Chen's supporters wanted to break with what they often contemptuously referred to the "political fiction" of Taiwan being part of China.

"We Are Taiwanese"

Indeed, for much of the democratization era, Prof. Jonathan Sullivan relates,

> "national identity was the major cleavage in Taiwanese society and the major fault line in Taiwanese politics. But after the apotheosis of Taiwanese identity during the rule of Chen Shui-bian, a period in which all politics and much governance was refracted through the lens of Taiwanese identity and

Chen imperative of Taiwanization, it has declined in salience in political discourse."[2]

"In Taiwan since the early 1990s, Taiwanese identity has rapidly supplanted Chinese identity," add Profs. Horowitz and Tan. "This has pushed all the main political parties to adopt policies favorable to the new identity, and brought the Democratic Progressive Party to power." In fact, the shift in identity has become glaringly obvious according to the study.

"A distinctly Taiwanese identity unfolded rapidly following Taiwan's democratization in the late 1980s. ...Consider the changes over time in the familiar polls asking if people identify themselves as Taiwanese, Chinese, or both. From 1992 to 2004, those that consider themselves to be only Taiwanese rose from 17.3 percent in 1992, to around 25 percent in the mid-1990s, to around 40 percent from 1999 to the present; whereas those that self-identify exclusively as Chinese fell from about 26 percent in the early 1990s, to around 20 percent in the mid-1990s, to a bit over 10 percent in late 2001, to 6.3 percent in June 2004."[3]

Yet, despite the apparent tilt in demographics, the Mainlanders, known as *Waishengren* (People from Other Provinces) and their children, still form a socially and politically significant bloc and role in contemporary Taiwan. Dr. Stephane Corcuff, a noted French scholar on Taiwan, adds, "There exists a Mainlander phenomenon in Taiwanese society and polity." He adds that while this Mainlander force is strong, "the major political fault line within the Taiwanese society today does not seem to lie along the *Waishengren–Taiwanese* divide."[4]

> *Who's Who? Chinese, Taiwanese, Aborigine* Contrary to myth, Taiwan's rich ethnic diversity reflects the island's stormy history. Nine major indigenous tribes are native to Taiwan. Each indigenous group has its own tribal languages which are Formosan and belong to the Proto-Austronesian linguistic family. The Ami, Paiwan, Atayal, and the Yami are some of the groups. In 1997, the number of indigenous people living on the island was 389,000, about 2.3 percent of the population of 22 million. Most of the tribes live in the rugged mountain regions. Today, Taiwan aboriginal residents number 540,000. The largest number of Mainland Chinese came to Taiwan after the fall of the Nationalists in 1949. The *Waishengren* (People from Other Provinces) included soldiers, civil servants, and some

> fleeing families from the civil war. Though a minority of about 12 percent, this bloc and their children were long wedded to the KMT and have been largely pro-unification and a backbone of ROC identity. The Mainlanders have been disproportionally influential in Taiwan especially up to 2000. The "Taiwanese" form the majority whose ancestors came from coastal provinces such as Fukien centuries ago. Though they have a distinct identity, the Hokko and the Hakka, originally from coastal China are nonetheless Han Chinese as much as is the Mainlander minority. During the Chen's DPP administration, there was a distinct *Taiwanization* movement. Despite the political undertones, intermarriage between both Mainlanders and Taiwanese today is quite common.
> Sources: 1999 Republic of China Yearbook (Taipei: GIO, 1999), pp. 27–31. "Supporters of Unification and the Taiwanization Movement," Stephane Corcuff, 2007, China Post 16 February 2015, p. 4.

During the DPP administration, Taiwan's once vibrant economy began to noticeably downshift to slower growth rates and declining economic confidence. The impressive development of the past seemed a memory and Taiwan appeared to lose some of its old dynamism. Blatant corruption, part of the KMT political landscape, returned and took its toll on the social system.

From 2001 to 2004, Taiwan's growth slowed to an anemic 2.7 percent while unemployment jumped to 4.8 percent. Such statistics reflected both a political uncertainty from Chen's administration and a decline in global growth in the wake of the September 2001 terrorist attacks on the USA.

Indeed, during Chen's two terms, the ROC's average economic growth reached 3.4 percent between 2000 and 2009. Most troubling was the precipitous rise in unemployment. While joblessness reached a new high of 2.6 percent in 1996, it remained basically unchanged despite the 1997 Asian Economic Crisis, not to mention the Taiwan earthquake in September 1999, unemployment jumped to 4.6 percent in 2001 and to 5 percent in 2002. Later in Chen's tenure, the jobless rate sank to 3.9 percent in 2007.[5]

Relations with Mainland China presented the DPP administration with a particular paradox.

On the one hand, President Chen's government was politically wary of the People's Republic, especially the deep economic ties which had developed during the previous administration in the 1990s. Equally, Chen's emphasis on the Taiwanese identity and the downplaying of the Chinese heritage would logically work to distance, if not strain, any widening socio-economic ties between both sides of the Taiwan Strait. Given the rush to do business on the Mainland, the "cooling off period" counseled by Chen was both prudent and politically savvy.

Taiwan's trade and investment in China had grown exponentially. In 1999, two-way trade stood at $26 billion. According to the Ministry of Economic Affairs in Taipei, in 2000 the trade reached $32 billion with a huge surplus in Taiwan's favor; by 2009, two-way trade reached $109 billion with a $58 billion surplus flying into Taipei's coffers.[6]

Taiwan has importantly stressed the role and value of high technology as a leading edge in its economy. A number of world-class Science Parks such as Hsinchu have long served as a base for innovation and development. Chipmakers such as Taiwan Semiconductor and United Microelectronics Corporation are among over 400 companies in the park. In 2004, over $32 billion in business was generated at Hsinchu. Significantly though, many of Taiwan's Information Technology companies were equally invested in manufacturing high-tech products on the Mainland. While places like Hsinchu profit from Taiwan's research and development (R&D)-rich technological environment, the same companies are using Mainland Chinese production facilities.

Despite their long-standing political estrangement since 1949, Taiwan and the PRC set out to find a common commercial bottom line to promote business. This was only logical given that both Chinese-speaking states reflected an entrepreneurial culture as well as proximity. Yet, reflecting the law of unintended consequences, such commerce edged Taiwan into a trading dependence on its erstwhile foe.

At the same time, Taiwan's business ties with China were growing, with expanding commercial ties between Taiwan and Mainland China increasing dependence of Taiwan's economy on China. Large numbers of Taiwan businessmen came to reside in China as well. Cross allegiances re-emerged among the original "Mainlander" families living in Taiwan but who also retained significant business interests on the Mainland.

Former President Richard Nixon advised, "Like a couple who have gone through a bitter divorce, China and Taiwan have irreconcilable differences. The separation is permanent politically but they are in bed together economically; they need each other. ... Taiwan is rapidly becoming China's biggest foreign investor. A more prosperous Taiwan sees China's interests. A more prosperous China serves Taiwan's interests." The former president then offered a piece of geopolitical advice as well: "The best guarantee of Taiwan's security is our relationship with the People's Republic of China. The Chinese will not launch a military attack against Taiwan as long as Beijing knows such an action would jeopardize their relationship with the United States."[7]

Chen's inaugural address in May extended an olive branch to Beijing:

> Therefore as long as the CCP regime has no intention to use military force against Taiwan, I pledge that during my term in office, I will not declare independence, I will not change the national title, I will not push forth the inclusion of the so-called 'state to state' description in the Constitution, and I will not promote a referendum to change the status quo in regards to independence or unification.

Chen went so far as to assert: "Under the leadership of Mr. Deng Xiaoping and Mr. Jiang Zemin, the mainland has created a miracle of economic openness. In Taiwan, over a half century, not only have we created a miracle economy, we have also created the political marvel of democracy." He stressed that with "goodwill reconciliation, active cooperation, and permanent peace" both sides "will also create a glorious civilization for the world's humanity."[8]

Equally, the DPP resolved its pro-independence platform and its current goal was to maintain Taiwan's *status quo*, stated the party's Chairman Frank Hsieh. He stressed, "our current strategy and attitude toward the pro-independence platform already differs from those of the early years of our party ... today we recognize that Taiwan is already an independent sovereign state formally known as the Republic of China." Hsieh added the ruling DPP would defend Taiwan's *status quo*.[9]

Yet, before long Beijing's political bromides flowed forth criticizing the newly elected president. A commentary, entitled "Opposing 'Taiwan Independence' and Promoting Reunification," the state-run *Xinhua* news agency correspondents opined, "The words and deeds of the leader of the Taiwan authorities make it impossible to mitigate people's misgivings about his creation of 'Taiwan independence' and his following the 'Lee

Teng-hui's line without a Lee Teng-hui." Some other chieftains of the Taiwan authorities have further openly turned themselves into one of the sources of tension in Cross–Strait relation and political and economic turbulence on the island with their 'Taiwan independence' words and deeds." The editorial held special contempt for Taiwan's vice president; "Annette Lu echoes with the extreme 'Taiwan independence' forces in the island, dishing out separatist fallacies, such as the so-called the two banks of the Straits are 'distant relatives and near neighbor' 'acknowledging one China is tantamount to surrender,' 'not taking about the 'two-states theory' is not tantamount to its non-existence."[10]

While there was no doubt that DPP's ideological traditions clearly favored Taiwan independence, President Chen's accession to power ensured that the reality of governance meant that party's political sails would be trimmed in the medium term at least. Naturally, the PRC was looking for any rhetorical scintilla of separatism, of which there were many in the DPP's vocal membership, with which to criticize and threaten Taiwan. While Chen, a practiced lawyer, was not too rash as to try to provoke the PRC, he was after all an elected official whose mandate rested on delivering a very different vision of the ROC/Taiwan to the constituents. Balancing Beijing's ire with the responsibilities of governing a free-wheeling democracy was the narrow path Chen would tread.

At the same time, Chen's DPP was pushing to gain international space for Taiwan despite a global diplomatic onslaught by Beijing. The UN became the venue for a renewed ROC effort to regain the seat and membership lost back in October 1971. In fact in 1993, the KMT had launched a number of political trial balloons to regain the "China Seat" for Taiwan. Reflecting the global climate of new members resulting from the collapse of the Soviet Union and former Yugoslavia, more than 15 new member states, Taipei looked to ride the wave of change and press for some form of UN participation.

Beijing would not budge on the issue. Yet, Taiwan's Foreign Ministry and overworked unofficial delegation in New York were tasked to come up with what could only be described as novel and creative approaches to try to crack this diplomatic diamond of UN participation; a path to promote Taiwan's identity and at the same time offer a fair compromise for the island's participation. In 2001, a letter by ten of Taipei's diplomatic allies requested a supplementary agenda item for the General Assembly's annual session. The item stated: "Need to examine the Exceptional international situation pertaining to the Republic of China on Taiwan, to ensure that the fundamental rights of its twenty-three million people to participate in the work and activities of the United Nations is fully respected." Beijing summarily blocked the move in committee. Nonetheless, during the General Assembly debate, shadowed by the September 11th attacks on the USA, 18 of Taipei's allies publicly raised the issue of Taiwan's participation from the marble rostrum of the General Assembly.[11]

In 2002 and 2003, Chen instituted a campaign to approve a referendum process for the island's voters. Though seemingly a manifestation of wider democracy, the DPP favored referendums for key national issues, such as constitutional reform, participation in international organizations, and national security. Critics both in the PRC and in the KMT, and the increasingly nervous US State Department saw the referendum process as a thinly veiled exercise of an eventual vote on Taiwan independence. By the end of 2003, the legislature passed a bill allowing for referendums but with the careful caveats that such votes could not be held on the changing of the Taiwan's flag or Taiwan's official name, the Republic of China. The first referendum was scheduled to coincide with the presidential election voting in March 2004.

Presidential Elections

With Presidential elections looming, the political showdown looked strikingly similar to 2000.

The DPP government party, and the Taiwan Solidarity Union (TSU) of the former president Lee Teng-hui represented the "Green Camp" symbolizing Taiwanese identity.

The "Blue Camp" or Pan Blue representing Chinese ethnicity comprised the KMT Nationalists, the People First Party (PFP), and the New Party.

On the DPP slate, Chen Shui-bian would run for president along with Annette Lu for vice president. For the KMT, Lien Chan would again run for president with PFP's James Soong running for vice president. While the names were the same as in 2000, the fateful split of the Nationalists was averted. With a presumably united front, the Nationalists stood a good chance to win, especially in the wake of the DPP's poor economic performance and lingering questions about whether the party would hold to the preferred *status quo* or make risky moves along the separatist path. A still mysterious event a day before polling changed the already razor-thin political calculus. While riding in open vehicle during a campaign event, both President Chen and Annette Lu were shot by an unknown gunman.

Fortunately, neither Chen nor Lu was hurt seriously. Yet, a "sympathy turnout" from the event may have helped the DPP duo win.

When ballots were counted, the Chen–Lu ticket won 6,471,970 votes, or 50.11 percent. The Lien–Soong team won 6,442,452, or 49.89 percent. The DPP won by a margin of 29,518 votes or 0.22 percent of the electorate. Results of the first referendum were an afterthought; the questions on missile defense and equal negotiation with the Mainland saw 90 percent plus votes but the measures failed to reach the required 50 percent of total turnout and the questions fell by the wayside.[12]

Newly re-elected, Chen Shiu-bin became more prone to assert Taiwan identity. The Pan Blue camp was bitter but soon resigned to the outcome of the vote. Trying times were on the near horizon.

Based on what they viewed as a "mandate" in their presidential victory in March, the Pan Green leaders projected substantial gains in the Legislative elections slated for December. Gaining legislative control would allow the DPP to push for and gain its more controversial political platform free of KMT filibustering. "In December 2004, Chen pledged that after the elections he would replace 'China' with 'Taiwan' in the official names of Taiwan's state-owned enterprises, embassies, and overseas missions," according to Kerry Tombaugh in a CRS report to Congress.

Many pre-election polls predicted that the December 11 election would be won by the DPP. The outcome was thus a shock when the KMT retained a slight legislative majority and control. But in what was clearly a shock to DPP/TSU party leaders, the opposition KMT retained slight legislative control with 114 members and the DPP coalition 101 members, with the remaining 10 seats in the 225 member body held by independents. DPP moderates blamed the setback on President Chen's "radically pro-independent" campaign rhetoric, and in a bow to this criticism, Chen resigned as DPP party chairman on 15 December 2004.[13]

Already in Chen's first term, there was a clear and perceptible Taiwanization of many names, the political lexicon, and national identity. The government publication *Free China Weekly* was changed to *Taiwan Journal*. Banknotes designs evolved as well where the 500 New Taiwan Dollar (NT) note had a design of the cheering Taiwan *Little League* team on the obverse and a group of deer on the reverse; the 1000 NT note showed school children looking at a world globe while the reverse had a pheasant. The DPP government dared not change the high usage 100 NT note with the iconic portrait of Dr. Sun Yat-sen nor the 200 NT note with a portrait of Chiang Kai-shek. Yet, the *tilt to Taiwanese identity away from Chinese identity was obvious.*

As part of the rites of autumn, Taipei's allies drafted a request which encompassed a persuasive ten-page position paper on what Taiwan is doing and can do to help the global community on the humanitarian front. In 2004, "Question of the representation of the twenty-three million people of Taiwan in the United Nations," 15 of Taipei's allies presented the case. China's delegate Wang Guangya thundered back, "The issue of China's representation in the United Nations was long solved once and for all in political, legal and procedural terms ... therefore, there is simply noise as the so-called 'Taiwan's representation in the United Nations.' Any attempt to distort or even deny the UNGA resolution 2758 (XXVI) is futile."[14]

Despite the unmistakable Taiwanization tilt, both Chen Shui-bian and opposition figure James Soong of the PFP held a landmark February meeting in which Chen stated clearly that he "will not declare independence and will not change the national moniker."[15]

In March 2005, the National People's Congress, Beijing's rubber-stamp legislature, enacted China's "Anti-Secession Law," of which Article 1 states clearly: "This Law is formulated, in accordance with the Constitution, for the purpose of opposing and checking Taiwan's secession from China by secessionists in the name of "Taiwan independence," promoting peaceful national reunification, maintaining peace and stability in the Taiwan Strait, preserving China's sovereignty and territorial integrity, and safeguarding the fundamental interests of the Chinese nation." Article 2 adds predictably, "There is only one China in the world. Both the Mainland and Taiwan belong to one China." After citing the benefits of reunification under Beijing's parameters, the law then warns that should "Taiwan independence secessionist forces should act under any other name or by any means to cause the fact of Taiwan's secession from China ... the Stare Council and Central Military Commission shall decide on and execute by non-peaceful means any other necessary measures," to deal with the situation. The clear reference to "non-peaceful means," for example, the use of military force, remained an ominous red line across the Taiwan Strait.[16]

Article 8 asserts that the PRC would resort to "non-peaceful means" if "major incidents entailing Taiwan's secession" occur. A US Congressional report on China states candidly: "The ambiguity of these 'red lines' appears deliberate allowing Beijing the flexibility to determine the nature, timing and form of its response. Added to this atmosphere of ambiguity are political factors internal to the regime in Beijing that might affect its decision-making but are opaque to outsiders."[17]

> *Anti-Secession Law 2005* Responding to secessionist rumblings in Taipei, in March of 2005, the National People's Congress, the PRC's rubber-stamp assembly, passed the controversial "Anti-Secession Law." Basically the edict draws a red line across the Strait. Article 2 states clearly, "There is only one China in the world. Both the mainland and Taiwan belong to one China." *Article 8* adds menacingly, "in the event that the 'Taiwan independence' secessionist forces should act under any name or by any means cause the fact of Taiwan's secession from China, or that major incidents entailing Taiwan's secession from China should occur, or that possibilities for a peaceful reunification should be completely exhausted, the state shall employ non-peaceful means and other necessary measures to protect China's sovereignty and territorial integrity." The State Council and the Central Military Commission shall decide on and execute the non-peaceful means and other necessary measures."
> *Source*: China-USC.edu

Though most of the world press chastised China's unmistakable military threat to democratic Taiwan, at the same time, the "Anti-Secession Law" spelled out dire consequences for the ROC, a country which is recalled, did not have any defensive military treaties as does South Korea.

ANTI-SECESSION LAW

Just a month after the "Anti-Secession Law," another political thunderclap rocked the Strait.

Kuomintang Chairman Lien Chan arrived in China for a controversial and historic "journey of peace." The eight-day visit "marked the first KMT leader to set foot on the Mainland since his party lost a civil war to the communists and fled the island in 1949," according to the *China Post*.

Lien said, "I left the mainland 59 years ago. It's a long period of time." Lien met with the PRC leader Hu Jintao. Lien, though a former ROC premier and vice president, lost two bids for the presidency in 2000 and just a year earlier in 2004.[18]

Thus, during the fall of 2005, Chen's administration was entering dangerous waters. China's precipitous military buildup gave the DPP government particular cause for concern. The PRC's "Anti-Secession Law" had moreover written a stark red line in policy. Chen's National Day address stressed, "Taiwan's security offers the only protection for the safeguard of Taiwan's life, liberty and property. ... We cannot expect to rely on others for Taiwan's self defense." He added, "China's suppression of Taiwan in the international community and its deployment of missiles to imperil Taiwan's national security constitute not only threats to a democratic and free Taiwan, but also challenge the global community and democracies," he implored. At the same time, Chen pressed for additional weapons purchases from the USA, programs which were stalled by the opposition party in the legislature. The speech did not give any hints or support for a separatist path for the island.[19]

The separatist agenda was temporarily sidelined due to a series of scandals bedeviling the DPP administration. At the same time, public opinion polls saw the president's popularity fall to a new low of 25 percent, his poorest performance rating since taking office in 2000. Chen, whose popularity reached 79 percent shortly after he became president, was hurt by both a poor economy and a spate of corruption scandals, the most obvious dealing with DPP officials profiting from contracts in the Kaohsiung rapid transit system. Equally, the DPP party also saw a plunge in popularity with a 24 percent rating in a *United Daily News* poll. Yet, the polling showed a maturity in the electorate; the opposition *Pan Blue* parties did not fare that much better. The KMT had an approval of 35 percent while the PFP gained only 20 percent in approval.[20]

Taiwan had experienced its first negative growth rate since 1945 and unemployment was ticking upward. Though part of the problem rested in the bursting of the Internet bubble as well as the aftereffects of 2001 terrorist attacks in the USA, part of the blame could also be put on a DPP administration which was sending mixed and confusing political and economic signals.

At the same time, during the December elections for county magistrates, township chiefs, and city majors, the KMT trounced the ruling coalition on all three levels. The vote was seen as a serious domestic setback to President Chen and the Pan Green alliance.

In a New-year message for 2006, Chen Shui-bian went on the political offensive, reigniting the core DPP values of Taiwanese identity. He spoke of a

> "Taiwan Consciousness, viewed as a taboo by the immigrant regime of our past to gradually take root on this land and to thrive in the hearts of our people. The Taiwan Consciousness breaks away from the shackles of historical bondage and political dogma and is founded upon the 23 million people of Taiwan's own self recognition. ... With no clear national identity, our national security cannot be safeguarded, for there will be no basis upon which national interests can be defended. Hence we must persevere to uphold Taiwan Consciousness and urge both the governing and opposition parties to rise above the unification-independence conflict, to see beyond issues of ethnicity, and work in the common interest so as to garner a consensus on national identity."

The speech also returned to the controversial issue to "produce Taiwan's new constitution by 2008; one that is timely, relevant and viable." He went on to say, "Who is to say that holding a referendum on the new Constitution by 2007 is an impossibility? After all this is an overarching national goal of Taiwan."[21]

Though Taiwan Consciousness has many meanings, the reference "viewed as a taboo by the immigrant regime of our past," although being true, presented a direct affront to the KMT Nationalists, to the Mainlanders who came to Taiwan after WWII, and to the dignity of the Republic of China. The address, while marking the formal anniversary of the Republic of China in 1912, specifically concentrated on the Taiwanese identity and the Taiwan Consciousness movement. The aspiration and dream to replace the Republic of China Constitution (dating to 1947) and to "produce Taiwan new Constitution by 2008" presented a specific name change in the *de jure* title and legal personality of the Republic of China. Though a deliberate rhetorical slight, the statements caused deep concern with both the opposition parties and the Beijing rulers.

Commemorating the tragic but complex events surrounding Taiwan's 28 February 1947 incident allowed President Chen to keep the pot simmering. Publication of a special report on the serious civil disorders which rocked the island early in Nationalist rule in which thousands may have died reopened debate on a justifiably contentious issue. Though a commemorative holiday was first enacted during Lee Teng-hui's tenure, 28th February took on a special meaning for many Taiwanese who were marginalized during the early stages of ROC rule. The report by the 28th

February Memorial Foundation concluded that Chiang Kai-shek was the "chief culprit" of the massacre that followed riots and a subsequent military crackdown on the island. Three other culprits were named, including the infamous Governor Chen Yi. President Chen, speaking at a meeting to mark the publication, stated that the "truth can heal" but added that the former ROC leader Chiang Kai-shek should be remembered as the main culprit. KMT legislators, former officials, and many Mainlanders were furious over placing the specific blame on the former ROC president who was still in Nanking, China, at the time of the disturbances.[22]

A month later, Chen Shui-bian stirred anger across the Straits with the intention to scrap the government's National Unification Council and the guidelines for Unification, which, while largely symbolic, soon became a flashpoint with PRC President Hu Jintao calling the move a "grave provocation." The moves, seen as a bow to the DPP stalwarts, riled both Beijing and Washington. The Bush Administration pressured Chen to soften the wording from "abolish" to "cease to function." The US State Department was able to gain this very nominal concession from Chen. Despite the nuance of the statements, the move clearly threatened the *status quo* and was proof that despite Washington's objections the USA could not constrain Chen's political tactics.[23]

Meanwhile on the diplomatic front, in 2006, another attempt was made to gain UN participation. Supported by 16 states, the measure was called, "Question of the Representation and participation of the 23 million people of Taiwan in the United Nations." Part of the presentation's supporting data related that Chen Shui-bian advised an international video press conference, "Should it accept Taiwan, the United Nations would certainly provide a most effective international monitoring mechanism for the development of a framework of peace and stability between the two sides of the Strait. Indeed, it would be able to exercise a decisive influence on peace in the Taiwan Strait and the security of the Asia-Pacific region." The move was stillborn.[24]

Domestically however, "The number of presidential associates in trouble with the law ballooned in 2006," added Prof. Shelly Rigger, "and prosecutors turned their attention to Chen's family." In May, his son-in-law was arrested in a swirl of rumors that Chen's wife, "Wu Shu-jen, was involved in insider trading and influence peddling." Rigger added, "The scandals undermined Chen's effectiveness and eroded his popular support. A wave of disgust was rising even among DPP activists." She adds, "The rest of Chen's term passed in a blur of corruption allegations, indictments, trials and recriminations."[25]

By 2007 the political clock was ticking on the last full year of Chen's DPP Administration.

The massive Chiang Kai-shek Memorial Hall in the center of Taipei presented the perfect setting for another round of Chen's histrionics. The hall, constructed between 1976 and 1980, was the historical centerpiece of a grand series of Chinese-styled structures including the performing arts center and a park. Chen and the DPP decided to rename the Chiang Kai-shek Memorial despite the fact that only the national Legislature could do so. Nonetheless, Chen had two giant banners unfurled proclaiming the name "National Taiwan Democracy Memorial Hall." There was an immediate backlash; the Taipei Mayor Hau Lung-bin spearheaded a drive in the municipal council to restore, actually uncover, the original name. In an operation evoking military planning, the banners were swiftly removed. The *China Post* commented editorially: "The people of Taiwan are not so naive as to have forgotten Chiang's mistakes, but by and large, have decided to honor the Generalissimo's contributions to history and to Taiwan. Put quite simply, most of the residents of the democratic island of Taiwan do not wish to see the CKS Hall changed."[26]

Though it was painfully obvious that membership attempts for the ROC/Taiwan were facing political checkmate from the People's Republic, President Chen decided in the last year of his tenure to make a politically motivated gamble for admission to the world body. On 19 July 2007, Chen Shui-bian wrote to UN Secretary General Ban Ki-moon making a direct application for Taiwan's membership. There was no mention of the *de jure* name Republic of China or any allusion to the legal name of this former UN member state. The UN Secretary General returned Chen's letter without comment. Under a separate Request, 14 of Taipei's allies sent a letter "urging the Security Council to process Taiwan's membership application pursuant to rules 59 and 60 of the provisional rules of procedure of the Security Council and Article 4 of the Charter of the United Nations." The attached draft resolution set off a political firestorm both with Beijing and Taiwan's opposition Nationalist (KMT) party; "welcoming the membership application by the Taiwan Government." Nowhere in the text of the draft resolution was there any mention of Republic of China.[27]

Chen Shui-bian's fractious tenure is probably best remembered for two things: the emergence of Taiwan Consciousness and its ensuing political ramifications for separatism, and the strained relations with Washington. During this period, the Bush administration, despite its initial enthusiasm, saying early in Chen's tenure that the USA "will do whatever it takes" to defend Taiwan, soon became decidedly nervous about being inadvertently pulled into a military conflict in the Pacific. While politically supporting Taiwan, the American administration made it increasingly clear that Washington would not sanction Taiwan separatism nor formal independence. Thus, Chen's DPP became increasingly distanced from its "informal ally" and major political partner in the USA.

Professor Sullivan opines, "But after the apotheosis of Taiwanese identity during the rule of Chen Shui-bian, a period in which all politics and much governance was refracted through the lens of Taiwanese identity and Chen's imperative of Taiwanization, it has declined in salience in political discourse." He added, "The traumatic unraveling of Chen's eight years in power, which culminated in the DPP's devastating electoral performances in 2008 and a jail term for corruption for Chen, led to period of retrenchment and internal debate about the role of Taiwanese identity in the party's platform."[28]

Notes

1. Op. cit. Why Taiwan Matters, p. 80.
2. Jonathan Sullivan. Taiwan's Identity Crisis The National Interest, August 2014.
3. Horowitz and Tan. The Strategic Logic of Taiwanization, World Affairs Vol. 168 No. 2 (Fall 2005), pp. 87–95.
4. "Supporters of Unification and the Taiwanization Movement," Stephane Corcuff China Perspectives 2004, 53, pp. 49–65.
5. Economic Development ROC/Taiwan Council for Economic Planning 2010, pp. 15, 34.
6. Development of International Trade in the Republic of China (Taiwan) 2011. Bureau of Foreign Trade Ministry of Economic Affairs. p. 11.
7. Richard M. Nixon. Beyond Peace (New York: Random House, 1994), p. 134.
8. Transcript of Chen Shui-bian Inauguration speech May 20, 2000, FAS.org
9. DPP Does Not Rule Out 'Unification' as Option for Taiwan's Future Sept 6, 2000 CNA Taipei, FAS.org
10. "Opposing 'Taiwan Independence' and Promoting Reunification," written by Xinhua Correspondents Fan Liqing and Chen Binhua Xinhua 28 December 2000 FAS.org

11. UNGA A/56/193 8 August 2001.
12. "Taiwan's Presidential Election in 2004; It's Impact on PRC-Taiwan Relations" SOAS London April 2004.
13. Kerry Dumbaugh. Taiwan in 2004: Elections, Referenda and Other Democratic Challenges. CRS Report to Congress, January 2005, p. 4.
14. UNGA A/59/194 10 August 2004 and PRC Press/UN Statement by H.E. Ambassador Wang Guangya 15 September 2004.
15. "President says He Will Not Seek Independence," China Post 25 February 2005, p. 1.
16. "Anti-Secession Law Adopted by NPC," 14 March 2005, USC US-China Institute, china-usc.edu.
17. "Military Power of the People's Republic of China 2008/Annual Report to Congress." Office of the Secretary of Defense Washington DC, 2008, p. 41.
18. "Lien in China for Historic Trip," China Post 27 April 2005, p. 1.
19. China Post 11 October 2005, pp. 1–2.
20. China Post 10 October 2005, p. 1.
21. Taiwan Journal 6 January 2006, pp. 1, 7.
22. "228 Report 'Truth that can heal,' President Chen," China Post 20 February 2006, p. 1.
23. "Beijing Accuses Taiwan Leader of 'Grave provocation." New York Times 1 March 2006, p. A11.
24. UNGA A/61/194 11 August 2006.
25. op. cit. Why Taiwan Matters, pp. 88–89.
26. "War Over 'Memorial Hall' name Escalates," China Post 23 May 2007, pp. 1–2.
27. UNGA A/62/193 17 August 2007.
28. op. cit. "Taiwan's Identity Crisis."

CHAPTER 7

Taiwan/Republic of China 2008–2016

Ma Ying-jeou, a Nationalist Party (KMT) pragmatist, overwhelmingly won the 2008 presidential elections. The poll result saw Ma's KMT garner 58 percent of the vote as compared to the DPP's 42 percent. As the old adage is often said about elections, "It's the economy stupid."

Indeed a growing economic malaise began to show on the once prosperous island. Taiwan's *per capita* income was surpassed by South Korea, a psychological milestone, which drove home the point. And without question, certain Mainland Chinese cities, such as Shanghai, were beginning to look like Taipei.

Ma, a successful Taipei mayor, was challenged on a wider scale as he entered the Executive Mansion. Taiwan's increasingly isolated and perilous security position in the world became a deep concern. The vote nonetheless sent a clear signal that Taiwan's 23 million did not wish to roil the proverbial political waters of the Taiwan Strait. They wanted to retain the *status quo* and the ensuing economic prosperity.

Ma's inaugural address "Taiwan Renaissance" opened new vistas for the island but equally moored policy to a clear and unambiguous pursuit of peace across the Taiwan Strait. Ma, a Harvard trained lawyer, stated his administration's position; "I sincerely hope that the two sides of the Taiwan Strait can seize this historic opportunity to achieve peace and co-prosperity. Under the principle of 'no unification, no independence, and no use of force' as Taiwan's mainstream public opinion holds it, and under the framework of the ROC Constitution, we will maintain the status quo in the Taiwan Strait." He added significantly, "In 1992, the two sides reached a consensus on 'one China, respective interpretations.' Many rounds of negotiation were then completed, spurring the development of cross-strait relations. I want to reiterate that, based on the '1992 Consensus,' negotiations should resume at the earliest time possible."[1]

On the sensitive issue of Taiwan's international status, Ma elaborated, "We will also enter consultations with mainland China over Taiwan's international space and a possible cross-strait peace accord. Taiwan doesn't just want security and prosperity. It wants dignity. Only when Taiwan is no longer being isolated in the international arena can cross strait relations move forward with confidence."

He equally evoked the political benediction of the founder of the ROC, Asia's first republic.

> Dr. Sun Yat-sen's dream for a constitutional democracy was not realized on the Chinese mainland, but today it has taken root, blossomed, and borne fruit in Taiwan.[2]

"Ma Ying-jeou's policies emphasize Taiwan's and China's shared interests; he aims to maximize the two sides economic complementarities," states Dr. Shelly Rigger, adding, "From the beginning of his presidency, he worked to improve Taiwan's relations with Beijing, both political and economic." Dr. Rigger advises, "But while Ma has never shared the Sinophobia that motivates Taiwan's Deep Green faction, it is Taiwan's interests—not unificationist ideology—that underlie his policies."[3]

Defusing a delicate situation with the People's Republic would not be simple especially given the rhetorical pyrotechnics of the Chen period. Ma made it clear that his government adhered to the one-China policy, also supported by Beijing, and the KMT was not going to push for separatism or sovereignty. At the same time, Ma achieved a diplomatic truce with PRC whereby neither side would poach the other allies.

For Taiwan safeguarding its diplomatic allies became a decidedly defensive game, but the point remained that Beijing would at least formally keep hands off places like Panama. For example, in 2007, Costa Rica, a longtime ROC ally, had switched recognition to Beijing: the price $300 million in PRC aid and debt relief. Still ROC Foreign Minister James Huang asserted that Taiwan would not enter a "checkbook diplomacy" battle with China. In the wider picture, a politically democratic and transparent Taiwan would no longer play a bidding game of dollar diplomacy for political allies.[4]

Seeing the setback with Costa Rica, one of Taipei's prime allies, President Ma knew a revised formula to protect Taiwan's remaining 23 allies from PRC "poaching" would need to be devised; the diplomatic truce with Beijing would offer such a formula.

An economic sea change of perceptions positively affected the economy in President Ma's first term. And despite the ill winds of the world economic recession not six months into his tenure, the economic improvements became tangible. While Taiwan's economic growth rate from 2000 to 2009 remained an anemic 3.4 percent, the overall economy was still a success story albeit without the supercharged statistics of the past. In 2009, growth still stood only at 1.9 percent but this reflected the downdraft in the global economy. In 2009, per capita income reached $16,353.

Taiwan's two-way trade reached an impressive $378 billion.[5]

Viewing trade, Mainland China (including Hong Kong) had become Taiwan's largest trading partner by 2009. Of the $378 billion in total trade, $109 billion or 29 percent was with the Mainland. More significantly, 41 percent of Taiwan exports went across the Strait to eager Mainland consumers and markets. The ROC on Taiwan had a $58 billion trade surplus with the PRC, making Taiwan increasingly dependent on the Mainland market. Japan, Association of South East Asian Nations (ASEAN), and the USA followed in this order, thus dramatically changing Taiwan trade patterns which in the past were heavily dependent on the USA and Japan. Two-way trade with the USA reached $42 billion in 2009, but the percentage of Taiwan exports to the USA has gradually decreased from 25 percent in 1999 to 11.6 percent in 2009. Despite the raw commercial numbers, one could equally deduce a subtle political shift as well.[6]

Just over a year into Ma's administration, a massive summer typhoon slammed into the island, causing severe flooding and damage in remote rural areas. Typhoon *Morakot* caused serious flooding and damage on Taiwan but equally challenged the new administration. While Ma's initial reaction to the crisis was not sure footed, especially in remote mountain regions where picturesque rivers and ravines became the scenes of rampant flooding and mudslides. Thus, the political perception, easily fueled in a hyper-sensitive situation where the affected ethnic population were largely indigenous inhabitants, was that Ma's ruling KMT did not really care about rural indigenous inhabitants. Though storm damage was not widespread island-wide, Taiwan's plethora of cable TV stations, replaying dramatic flooding footage in outlying areas, magnified the crisis turning Typhoon *Morakot* into a political disaster for Ma.[7]

At the UN, Taipei's policy tact trimmed its sails too. While the ROC continued to quietly pressure its allies to sponsor some sort of diplomatic formula for Taipei's "participation" in the UN, the tilt was toward specialized agencies, not formal General Assembly membership.

In 2008, Ma's first year, 17 of the ROC's diplomatic allies submitted a proposal, "Need to Examine the Fundamental Rights of the 23 million People of the Republic of China (Taiwan) to Participate Meaningfully in the Activities of the United Nations Specialized Agencies." The cautious move centered on specialized agencies such as the WHO, and the ICAO. Prior to 1971, the ROC participated actively in UN-specialized agencies. According to the Foreign Ministry in Taipei, "our appeal this year is pragmatic, flexible and non-confrontational, and is centered in participating meaningfully in the UN specialized agencies." Importantly too, in putting forth the case, the annual request used the *de jure* name Republic of China rather than Taiwan.[8]

During the UN General Assembly debate in September, a score of countries spoke of Taiwan's case from the rostrum of the Assembly. Though the tactic to switch the discussion from UN membership to a more flexible participation in specialized agencies failed to gain much traction in the full General Assembly, what did occur was a subtle shift whereby Beijing did not oppose Taipei's participation in the WHO as an observer. The breakthrough with Beijing allowed Taiwan's participation as an observer at the 2009 session of WHO's Geneva-based assembly.

Taiwan tried to join or at least participate in WHO's deliberations since 1997. Thus, with this guardedly optimistic switch, Taiwan's President Ma praised the invitation as showing "goodwill" from Beijing. Actually there was another very practical reason too.

> During the Asian SARS outbreak and again during the Avian flu pandemic in 2005–2006, both of which affected the Chinese Mainland and the island of Taiwan, cross–straits political gales trumped medical cooperation. People died and people suffered. Beijing's senseless isolation of Taiwan from WHO had deprived the East Asian region of Taiwan's advanced medical expertise. Taipei's participation as 'Chinese-Taipei' Observer means access to proceedings and prestige, but not voting rights or major policy input. The United States and Japan have long favored such an arrangement.[9]

Importantly, after 12 years of trying, Taipei achieved "Observer Status" in the WHO Assembly in 2009. Taiwan has now focused on joining other UN-specialized agencies such as ICAO in Montreal.

"Now there is a more pragmatic approach, a non-confrontational approach where our government looks to participate in UN specialized agencies," a ranking official of the ROC Foreign Ministry told the author. Stressing "meaningful participation" in the UN system, the Ma government favors a "pragmatic approach, building gradual support in different agencies." The "meaningful participation" approach as in the

WHO has been strongly supported by the USA, European Union, and Japan.[10]

The political template was outlined by Dr. Philip Yang, Minister of the ROC's Information Office, addressing the Asia Society, "Reconciliation between the two sides of the Taiwan Strait is helping Taiwan to expand its involvement in the international community. For example we have taken part in the World Health Assembly for three consecutive years as an Observer under the name 'Chinese Taipei.' We've also declared that Taiwan desires to participate in activities of the International Civil Aviation Organization and those in connection with the United Nations Framework Convention on Climate Change."[11]

During the UN Assembly, Panama's Vice President Francisco Alvarez de Soto stated,

> Panama, from the utmost respect to the existing diplomatic truce, calls for allowing greater participation from Taiwan in the forum and the international initiatives. ... Panama is one of twenty-three nations that recognize the Republic of China (Taiwan) and at the same time maintain harmonious commercial and cultural relations with the People's Republic of China, framed by Panama's respect for the current diplomatic truce.[12]

Prime Minister Ralph Gonsalves of St. Vincent and the Grenadines put the matter into elegant retrospect:

> As I reflect on the sweeping geopolitical changes being wrought in our global village, I am compelled to raise the fact that there is no practical, legal or logical justification for the UN's seeming indifference to the meaningful participation of Taiwan in our important work. ... Taiwan has proven herself to be a responsible global citizen, and a solid development partner in the fields of education, health, technology, agriculture and infrastructure." The Prime Minister added, "Amidst the howling winds of change that swirl around our international institutions, Taiwan's reasonable request is but a gentle breeze of inclusion and participation.[13]

The Ma administration scored a signature, if controversial, achievement with the Cross–Strait Economic Cooperation Framework Agreement (ECFA). The commercial logic was compelling as much as luring. Though Taiwan was a major trading partner with the world, the ROC lacked many formal Free Trade Agreements (FTA) with the ASEAN, the European Union, or the USA. Though its exports and imports had grown, Taiwan's trade as a share of global trade had gradually declined. The island was not part of 60 FTA agreements in Asia which lowered tariffs and thus was being excluded from growing regional economic integration. Taipei would attempt to sign the ECFA with Mainland China as a way to circumvent market barriers with its largest trading partner.

In 2010, two-way trade with Mainland China stood at $153 billion, amounting to 29 percent of Taiwan's total commerce. Significantly, the ROC enjoyed a $77 billion trade surplus with the PRC or three times its surplus with the rest of the world. Moreover, the Mainland was Taiwan's largest export market with $115 billion or 42 percent of the total; China was Taiwan's second largest source of imports at $38 billion or 15 percent of the total. Perhaps more significant, Mainland China was Taiwan's largest venue for investment with $101 billion or 61.5 percent of the total.[14]

Taiwan Trade 2015 Country List In 2015, Taiwan trade reached $509 billion, down from an impressive $588 billion the year before. Exports accounted for $280 billion while imports reached $229 billion. Bilateral trade with the People's Republic of China, Taiwan's number 1 trade partner, reached $115 billion, with $71 billion in exports from Taiwan and $44 billion in imports from the Mainland. Taiwan thus gained a $27 billion trade surplus with the Mainland.

Here are some two-way trade statistics for Taiwan:

Australia	$9 billion
Canada	$3.6 billion
France	$4 billion
Germany	$14.5 billion
India	$5 billion
Indonesia	$9 billion
Japan	$58 billion
Netherlands	$7 billion
Russia	$3.5 billion
Singapore	$24 billion
Thailand	$9.6 billion
UK	$5.6 billion
USA	$61 billion
Vietnam	$12 billion

Source: Bureau of Foreign Trade/ROC Taiwan. www.trade.gov.tw

Thus, in June 2010, the SEF and the ARATS signed the ECFA. The main objective of the ECFA is to seek fair treatment of Taiwan's products in the Mainland market. Despite serious misgivings from the DPP opposition, the ECFA came into effect in September 2010.

Commercially, transport and tourist ties are thriving between both sides of the politically estranged Chinese nation. Prior to 2008, flying between Taiwan and Chinese cities entailed stopovers and plane changes usually in Hong Kong. Naturally, such arrangements added to the time and cost.

By 2008, special "charter flights" around the time of Lunar New Year would soon expand to 36 weekly and soon 370 weekly between Taiwan and 37 different Chinese cities. By 2011, scheduled flights had reached 558 regular direct flights weekly. While ROC companies such as China Airlines (CAL) and EVA Air were major carriers, a plethora of Chinese regional carriers from Hainan Airlines to Dragon Air were ubiquitous both at the Taoyuan International Airport (the former Chiang Kai-shek International) to the downtown Songshan airport.

As President Ma stated during a 2013 video conference with Stanford University, "Five years ago there were no scheduled flights between Taiwan and the Mainland. Now there are 616 per week. Five years ago, 274,000 mainland people visited Taiwan. In 2012, there were 2.5 million people."[15]

Chinese tourists are commonplace in Taipei, whether visiting the extraordinary National Palace Museum or the historic National Martyrs Shrine. Surprisingly, the Chiang Kai-shek Memorial Hall holds a particular interest for mainland visitors. High-end shopping in the modern Taipei 101 skyscraper and a plethora of pricy boutiques cater to the cousins from across the Strait. The Grand Hotel, the magnificent Chinese architecture palace style jewel overlooking Taipei, is a popular destination. The Grand was long a nexus for foreign dignitaries and delegations going back to Chiang Kai-shek's era, its tall red columns and high ceilings evolving a palace and indeed presenting an aura. While revisiting the Grand, I saw the customary line of protocol officials, edgy photographers, and curious staff preparing to greet a delegation which I presumed was from one of Taiwan's Caribbean allies. A line of black limos and small busses soon arrived. The dark-suited delegation being feted was none other than the Provincial Governor of Hunan Province in the People's Republic of China.

Although many of the island's once ubiquitous statues and busts of the late leader Chiang Kai-shek were removed during the DPP era, the issue of the massive marble monument in central Taipei remained a political flashpoint. Though the Chen administration had renamed the building "National Taiwan Democracy Memorial Hall," back in 2007, the complex officially reverted to the original name "Chiang Kai-shek Memorial Hall," in July 2009. Nonetheless, as a balm to the opposition, the plaza outside retained the newer name "Liberty Square."[16]

In 2011, the Republic of China celebrated its centennial; the 100th anniversary of Sun Yat-sen's revolution which toppled the Manchu dynasty, subsequently creating Asia's first republic.

The anniversary was highlighted by military fighter jet flyovers and the traditional old-fashioned pomp and celebration of Double Ten day. Addressing a rally in Taipei, President Ma called on Mainland China to "face the fact" of the ROC's existence, "not in the past tense but the present." Indeed both Taiwan and the Mainland long engaged in a soft-power tug of war to claim the legitimate successor of Dr. Sun. In a stirring speech, Ma presented his doctrine on ROC–Taiwan relations in a sentence which was stated in Mandarin Chinese, Taiwanese, and Hakka. "The Republic of China is our nation and Taiwan is our home." He stressed that agreements with the Mainland conform to "the principles of parity, dignity, and reciprocity while putting Taiwan first."[17]

Ma's first term was about restarting the economy, maintaining the *status quo*, and moving the needle back to an, at least nominally, Chinese narrative. While never a popular president in the avuncular or media sense, and despite rifts within his own KMT party, Ma was able to run for and win a second term. The 2012 presidential election, despite the DPP's stronger challenge, saw the Ma ticket winning 51.6 percent of the vote versus the DPP's 45.6 percent. As in 2008, Taiwan's political landscape in 2012 reflected an island where Taipei, the north, and the center were backing the Nationalists, while the southwest and cities such as Kaohsiung and Tainan as well as the rural south voted predictably DPP.[18]

President Ma's second Inaugural Address offered a broad-brush picture of what he called a *Golden Decade* for the island, especially in the social, economic, and environmental spheres. Yet, the theme of Taiwan's creeping commercial isolation as well as a growing disparity in wages and social conditions was addressed. He equally stressed what he called "three legs" of National Security: Cross–Straits Peace, Viable Diplomacy, and a Strong Defense. "National security is crucial for the survival of the Republic of China. I believe Taiwan's security rests on three legs. The first is the use of cross-strait rapprochement to realize peace in the Taiwan Strait. The second is the use of viable diplomacy to establish more breathing space for ourselves in the international community. And the third is the use of military strength to deter external threats."

Addressing national security, Ma stated,

> In the area of weapons procurement from overseas, the United States has approved three arms sales to Taiwan since I took office, in aggregate totaling $18.3 billion, and exceeding all previous such sales in terms of quality and amount. This provides us with an appropriate defensive force in the future that will give the government and public a greater confidence and willingness to pursue continued stable and solid development of the cross-strait relationship.

Returning to the strong *Sino identity* theme, Ma stressed, "The people of the two sides of the strait share a common Chinese heritage. We share common blood lines, history, and culture. We both revere our nation's founding father Dr. Sun Yat-sen. ... Taiwan's experience in establishing democracy proves that it is not impossible for democratic institutions from abroad to take root in an ethnically Chinese society."[19]

The PRC side has been stressing another theme: "One China across the Strait" (lianganyizhong) seemed to have emerged as the main focus in China's quest for "deepening political trust."

According to Dr. Chao Chien-min,

> This policy was written into the CCP's political report at the 18th Party Congress held in November 2012. "The two sides should adhere resolutely to the common grounds of opposing 'Taiwan independence' and insisting on the '1992 consensus,' enhance common acknowledgement of one China framework and seek to maximize their commonalities and save differences on that basis." Built on the success of previous policies, the new Chinese leadership under Xi Jinping seems to have crafted a path of his own. The new policy is to stretch politics a bit more as nationalism creeps in as the core of Xi's ideology.

Dr. Chao adds, "Xi parroted the same tone orchestrated by his predecessor with more vigor," saying that "although not unified the two sides belong to the same China ... the two parties should insist on the stand of one China, and maintain the one China framework together ... the core of enhancing mutual trust is to consolidate and maintain one China principle so that a clear common acknowledgement can be formed."[20]

Security Issues

Taiwan continues to face a formidable and prepared military threat from the People's Republic of China. In 2014, Beijing announced a 9.3 percent military spending increase to $136 billion. Between 2005 and 2014, the PRC's officially disclosed military budget grew 9.5 percent. In comparison, PRC spending stands at $136 billion as compared to Taiwan's $10.3 billion.[21]

As part of the PRC's widening assertion of territorial claims, Beijing published an Air Defense Identification Zone (ADIZ) to cover the disputed Senkaku–Daoyutai islands. A Congressional report asserts, "In November 2013, China announced the creation of its ADIZ in the East China Sea with coverage that included airspace above the Senkaku Islands and that overlapped with previously established Japanese, South Korean and Taiwan ADIZ. Chinese officials have continued to publicly reiterate the claim that the islands are part of China's territory and that it will resolutely respond to any external provocation."[22]

"Security in the Taiwan Strait is largely a function of dynamic interactions between and among mainland China, Taiwan, and the United States. China's strategy toward Taiwan has been influenced by what it sees as positive developments in Taiwan's political situation and approach to engagement with China," asserts the study. Nonetheless should Taiwan cross the PRC's red lines of "Taiwan Independence" and what Beijing would describe as separatism, there is no doubt that the Chinese military would use a combination of naval blockade, seaplane harassment, or selective missile strikes against the island. "China might use a variety of disruptive, punitive, or lethal military actions in a limited campaign against Taiwan, likely in conjunction with overt and clandestine economic and political activities," the Report asserts.

Yet, at the same time, Taiwan's defensive advantage has narrowed in recent decades while the PRC military power projection potential has increased. The acute military preparedness that once characterized the ROC, making it a bit like the East Asian Israel, has considerably waned. "Taiwan is following through with its transition to a volunteer military and reducing its active military end-strength from 275,000 to approximately 175,000 personnel to create a "small but smart and strong force," cites the report.[23]

ROC defense spending has fallen in recent years, reaching a five-year low in 2011. "Despite an election promise by Ma to raise defense spending to 3 percent of GDP, only 2.2 percent of GDP was allowed to defense this year," stated a *Taipei Times* article. Defense spending has steadily dropped since 2008 according to DPP critics.[24]

With defense spending at 2.2 percent of GDP or $9.2 billion, Taiwan has actually slipped behind Singapore (with one-fifth of Taiwan's population) who spent $9.5 billion in 2011. Defense expert Su Tzu-yun advised that the balance of power against China, while spends ten times as much on its military than Taiwan "is skewed, and that invites aggression." He added, "The belief that economic cooperation prevents war is false," and that despite improving Cross–Strait relations, Taiwan needs to press for additional arms sales from the USA "or it risked sending the wrong signal."[25]

According to the *Military Balance*, the PRC military comprises 2.3 million (Army 1.6 million, Navy 235,000, Air Force 398,000, and Strategic Missile Forces 100,000.) The 12.2 percent increase in military spending in 2014 reflects PRC President Xi Jinxing's plans for both modernization and force projection. Taiwan maintains an active force of 290,000 (Army 200,000, Navy 45,000, and Air Force 45). Significantly, Reserves comprise 1.6 million. Though Taiwan has historically been outnumbered, the ROC's traditional advantages in quality systems, better training, and higher morale have eroded over the years. Efforts to acquire more modern F-16 C/D's from the USA has been delayed. At the same time, conscript service has been reduced to one year and conscription is slated to be phased out by 2017.[26]

The PRC's official defense spending of $129 billion in 2014 considerably overshadows Taiwan's $10.1 billion (which had declined from $10.45 billion in 2012). Viewed another way, Beijing's official military spending exceeds the combined totals of Australia, Japan, South Korea, the Philippines, Vietnam, and Taiwan.[27]

Given the staggering military imbalance, Taipei's policies need to focus on both deterrence and diplomacy. But viewing the wider picture, how do people on Taiwan, a thriving and often raucous democracy, actually feel about the pressing and rhetorically volatile issues of independence, unification, and the *status quo*? A periodic public opinion poll taken by the MAC and surveyed by Taipei's prestigious National Chengchi University offers a view into the political looking glass.

One such poll in May 2011 showed that 88 percent wish to keep the *status quo* in some form. Another 15 percent wish independence or immediate unification. Specifically, 32.6 percent support *status quo now/decision later*; 27.2 favor *status quo indefinitely*; while 19.2 percent wish for *status quo now/independence later*, and 9.4 percent *status quo now/unification later*. On the other side, 6.6 percent support *Independence ASAP*, while 0.8 percent wishes for *unification ASAP*. In another question, 46 percent of respondents said that the pace of Cross–Strait exchange *was just right* while 32.6 claimed it was *too fast*. Thirteen percent claimed it was *too slow*.[28]

This same poll "Public Views on Cross–Strait Relations," conducted in July 2014, related broadly similar themes. One such question "Do you think the Mainland Chinese government's attitude toward the government of the ROC to be friendly or unfriendly?" A total of 24.9 percent claimed friendly whereas 56 percent viewed it as unfriendly/very unfriendly. Nineteen percent had no opinion. When viewing the options toward *status quo*, independence, or unification, the numbers were fairly similar. Total 86.7 percent wished to keep the *status quo*, at least for now. Some 6.6 percent favored independence. More specifically, 31.8 percent supported the *maintaining the status quo now and deciding on independence or unification later*; 28.2 percent supported *maintaining the status quo indefinitely*; 20.1 percent wished for *status quo and independence later*; 6.6 percent declare *independence* as soon as possible; and 1.8 percent favoring *unification ASAP*. Only 4.9 percent held no opinion.[29]

Crisis Diplomacy

Ironically, a potential political flashpoint in the East China Sea allowed for Taipei and Beijing to share some common ground if only on a rocky atoll. The disputed Diaoyutai–Senkaku Islands, five uninhabited rocky islands and reefs just 100 miles northeast from Keelung port, have raised tensions been China and Japan in recent years. Though the islands were discovered and subsequently recognized as Chinese territory as early as the Qing Dynasty in 1683, the islands were seized by Japan in 1895. Following the Treaty of Shimonoseki, which stipulated that Qing China cede to Japan "the island of Formosa, together with all the islands appertaining or belonging to the said island of Formosa," the Daioyutai came under Tokyo's control. Yet, after Japan's defeat in 1945 and the return of Taiwan to the Republic of China, the nearby Ryukyu Islands were placed under US Trusteeship, the Daioyutai were placed under American administrative control, a status which conferred no sovereignty to them. As late as May 1971, US Secretary of State William Rogers stated that the USA took no position on the sovereignty issue and the dispute should be resolved through negotiations between the ROC and Japan.[30]

While the Diaoyutai–Senkaku crisis exhibited some dangerous confrontations between Chinese fishermen and Japanese Coast Guard vessels, the incidents gave rise to hyper nationalism in both Mainland China and Japan. Seemingly, small incidents could have led to wider posturing and subsequent confrontations at sea between the claimants. As would be expected, the PRC claimed the islands. Both Beijing and Taipei shared a general agreement that the islands were Chinese.

Though Taiwan was not directly involved in the rhetorical theatrics over the disputed atoll, President Ma took the political initiative to launch a Peace Plan for the Daoyutai. Fully aware that the sovereignty issue can take time to resolve, President Ma proposed a two-stage East China Sea Peace Plan in August 2012. While stressing that sovereignty is indivisible, resources can be shared. Thus, the Plan calls on the parties to replace confrontation with dialogue, and formulate a Code of Conduct and engage in joint development of resources. Thus, the Plan's Stage 1 is to shelve territorial disputes through meaningful dialogue; Stage 2 is to share resources through development. The ROC peace plan was largely overlooked by both the PRC and Japan.[31]

Despite having comfortably won two terms as ROC president, Ma Ying-jeou never seemed to sustain the personal popularity or magnetism needed to govern comfortably. Moreover, a political misstep concerning a trade services agreement with China caused both the Ma presidency and the KMT dearly in the court of public opinion. What was to be a signature piece of legislation for the president's second term, the Cross–Strait Services Trade Agreement triggered a domestic political typhoon in Taiwan. A move which planned at expanding and institutionalizing closer economic ties with the Mainland, instead caused a backlash.

In the wider context, Ma's commercial inclinations toward wider ties with China are viewed as a direct affront to many Taiwanese who view such business ties as a KMT ruse to smooth a path to reunification.

Student-led protests, known as the Sunflower Movement, brought a raucous demonstration to Taipei; the protesters soon seized the Legislative Yuan and created a chaotic showdown inside the Assembly Hall. Hundreds of demonstrators had stormed the Assembly, strung banners everywhere, and later encamped among the lawmakers' seats and rostrum. Under the gaze of the large Sun Yat-sen portrait, from mid-March to 10 April, the protesters issued demands to the government and the Assembly to put all agreements under close and careful scrutiny. The orchestrated chaos and disorder soon spread to a raucous assault and trashing of the nearby Executive Yuan. Police finally evicted the demonstrators. After much damage to the Assembly Hall, students decoded to withdraw and help clean up the mess. Though the Sunflower Movement showed deep frustration with elements of the political process, it was not specifically organized by the DPP opposition. Deep political unease over Ma's initially awkward handling of the Cross–Strait Services Trade Agreement had boiled over into the unpredictable Sunflower movement.[32]

But there is a wider issue too. The wealth gap and glaring economic disparities, which characterize many developing countries, such as the Philippines or Mainland China for that matter, were not nearly as pronounced during Taiwan's "economic miracle." Yet, given both globalization and the strong pull of the Mainland, there is "a new cleavage based on class has not just mitigated national identity, but has replaced it." Wu Yushan of Taiwan's Academia Sinica argues, "class politics based on wealth gap has become a new driving force of party politics … the dominant social cleavage has shifted away from identity towards distribution." Yet, as Prof. Jonathan Sullivan asserts, "Widespread dissatisfaction with Ma has mutated into disenchantment with politics and both major political parties."[33]

According to Prof. Shelly Rigger, "The deepest drivers of popular dissatisfaction in the past four years are the linked trends of declining economic security and growing anxiety about relations with the PRC. Since 2000, economic interdependence between Taiwan and the mainland has skyrocketed; the PRC is now Taiwan's top trading partner and investment destination. Many Taiwanese companies have profited enormously from this relationship and the country's GDP has grown faster than most of its peers. Nonetheless, the fruits of cross-Strait trade have not been shared evenly within Taiwan, and there is a strong perception that the middle class is being hollowed out and future opportunities lost because of over-reliance on the mainland."

"To make matters worse, many Taiwanese have become convinced that the extent of cross-Strait economic ties is making Taiwan vulnerable to Beijing's political interference," Rigger added.[34]

National Health Care Taiwan's compulsory National Health Insurance (NHI) plan has emerged as a success. Started in 1995 with the mission of providing universal health care, the NHI program is mandatory for all residents, including foreigners who reside on the island for more than four months. The program covers 99 percent of the population for outpatient care, lab tests, X rays, prescriptions, traditional medicine, and dental care. A key feature of the NHI program is a smartcard ID which not only provides access to medical services but stores an individual's medical history records, listing conditions, drug interactions, allergies, and so on. Premiums for NHI are based on 5.33 percent of taxable salary income. Importantly, patients have a free choice of health care providers.

Interestingly, Taiwan spends 6.6 percent of GNP on health, well below that of most developed states. Yet, Taiwan's health system is renowned worldwide. According to an HSBC Bank *Expat Explorer* Rankings, Taiwan offers affordable high-quality health care which is rated higher than systems in the UK, France, or obviously China. A Brookings report states "Taiwan's NHI may be said to be a high performing health care system compared with many other health care systems around the world. In terms of cost-effectiveness, Taiwan's system outperforms the U.S. system, which spends more than 17 percent of U.S. GDP." Tsung-mei Cheng adds, "One of Taiwan's strengths is its willingness to learn from other countries, and this extends to health policy makers—in contrast to U.S. health policy makers who show much greater reluctance to learn from systems abroad. The very creation of Taiwan's NHI, which is basically an amalgam of the Canadian health insurance system and the German method of financing health care, is such a manifestation."

One downside of the program is a growing shortage of medical doctors and nurses.

Source: "Taiwan's Health Care System: the Next Twenty Years," Tsung-mei Cheng, Taiwan/US Quarterly Analysis, #17 May 2015 and HSBC *Expat Explorer* rankings.

This backlash and overall *angst* was reflected in Taiwan's municipal and county elections held in the November 2014 elections. The so-called 9 in 1 elections were for over 11,000 public offices: mayors of the six major municipalities as well as a local and country posts. The KMT suffered a massive defeat at the hands of the voters with the ruling party only able to hold six of the 23 city and county governments, and only one of the six special municipalities. The DPP controls Taiyuan, Taichung, Tainan, and Kaohsiung. Taipei, long Nationalist stronghold, was won by an independent. The KMT only won in the New Taipei City. Turnout sent even a stronger message; 67.59 percent of the electorate voted. Following the electoral rebuke, the Premier and the Cabinet resigned while Ma Ying-jeou quit his post as KMT Chairman.[35]

The significant election setbacks for the ruling KMT did not argue well for the party's chances in the upcoming presidential elections in 2016.

Close commercial ties between Taiwan and the Mainland were part of the concern as much as the widening perception that Beijing had too strong an influence over the KMT government. President Ma tried to bring a balance to the argument stating that in 2014 the ratio of Taiwan exports to China has dropped to 39 percent. In 2000, China accounted for 24 percent of Taiwan exports while in 2008, the year Ma assumed office, the ratio was 40 percent. While trying to diversify exports, Ma stated that a close trade relationship between Taiwan and the Mainland is unavoidable in light of their geographic proximity.[36]

Indeed, China remains Taiwan's largest trading partner with two-way trade reaching $174 billion in 2014 ($130 billion PRC and $44 billion from Hong Kong). The USA stands as the ROC's second trade partner with $62 billion in two-way trade ($35 billion in exports and $27 billion in imports). Japan is Taiwan's third largest trading partner with $61.6 billion in bilateral commerce.[37]

Professor Robert Sutter opines that the Ma administration's conciliatory approach to Cross–Strait relations has actually exacerbated Taiwan's problem because it "reinforces ever-growing and deepening Chinese influence over Taiwan," economically, diplomatically, and militarily.

Richard Bush argues, "The economic interdependence that has grown between the two sides of the Strait evolves into Taiwan's dependence on the Mainland as its principal source of economic prosperity. ... China might seek to manipulate that dependence to 'encourage' Taiwan to accept a political settlement on its terms[38]."

> *Taiwan's Green Technology* The label "Made in Taiwan" has undergone a massive qualitative makeover. Incentives, Innovation, and Industrial capacity thrive in a number of specific high-tech Science Parks. Established in 1980, Hsinchu was the first and foremost of these science hubs which combine R&D with production. Taiwan excels in R&D with multinationals like Intel, Dell, HP, Sony, and IBM having facilities on the island.
>
> Hsinchu focuses on semiconductor and optoelectronics. Here, more than 520 companies employ more than 150,000 people. R&D accounts for 40 percent of Hsinchu's workforce with 60 percent of workers engaged in production. The largest IC Foundry provider TSMC, the second largest IC foundry provider UMC, the largest PC and branded PC maker Acer, among others, are in the Science Park. More than 70 percent of global IT industry products are initiated from firms at Hsinchu Science Park. Clustering of knowledge-based industries has been set up in a number of sites across the island starting in the 1990s. The Nankang Software Park founded in 1999, in Taipei, has focused on biotech and information software. The entire green island buzzes with high-tech industries and startups and Taipei has become a free Wi-Fi city. Wired Magazine once named Taipei City, the number 1 Digital City in Asia. Today, a *Taiwan Excellence* campaign is focused on marketing the island's high-tech and quality product image.
>
> Source: www.sipa.gov.tw

Regionally, Taiwan has a brisk and growing commerce with other nearby countries such as the Philippines. Two-way trade between Taipei and Manila jumped from $6 billion in 2009 to nearly $12 billion in 2014. But, with regard to bilateral trade, there are growing Taiwan investments, especially in green technology. Being the world's largest manufacturer of LED lighting, Taiwan firms have introduced such technology to the energy-starved Philippines. Other major Asian partners include Singapore at $29 billion, South Korea at $27 billion, and Malaysia at $17 billion.[39]

Yet, despite significant trade and warming if cautious rapprochement across the Strait, "China remains the No. 1 threat to Taiwan, even though it is also the nation's biggest opportunity," Taiwan's Representative to the USA Shen Lyu-shun stated. Addressing Philadelphia's Foreign Policy Research Institute (FPRI) Amb. Shen said, "China gives us better treatment for political reasons; they give our investors very good benefits." He added, "We need to minimize the stress and maximize the opportunity."[40]

As the 2016 Presidential elections approached, the ruling KMT and the outgoing Ma administration faced a revitalized DPP opposition. Contrary to uneasy memories of earlier DPP rule, and despite the enduring image of some opposition elements favoring outright Taiwan independence, the DPP nominee Tsai Ing-wen has staked out a moderate platform stressing the *status quo* rather than a politically disruptive image. In a speech before Washington's prestigious Center for Strategic and International Studies (CSIS), Tsai stressed that Taipei and Beijing should "treasure 20 years of exchanges" and stated clearly, "I am also committed to a consistent, predictable and sustainable relationship with China." Tsai stressed on "maintaining the status quo" and moreover added, "I will ensure that Taiwan works together with the U.S. to advance our common interests." Tsai's comments were a political balm to American nervousness during the stormy tenure of the earlier DPP administration.[41]

When Independent Taipei Mayor Ko Wen-je visited Shanghai, he avoided the political minefield of the 1992 consensus and instead stated the obvious, that the two sides of the Strait are "one family." An editorial in the opposition-leaning *Taipei Times* stated that his remark "has put a lot of pressure on the DPP, which staunchly opposes any 'one China' rhetoric. However, is this really the case? If Beijing can accept Ko's vague statements and his '2015 new standpoint,' it indicates that Ko has created a model of cross-strait interactions that lies outside the bounds of the nation's two-party spectrum." Indeed, as the editorial advised, "Cross-strait communication should not be monopolized by a single party."[42]

A landmark meeting between the KMT's Ma Ying-jeou and PRC President and Chinese Communist Party (CCP) Party chief Xi Jinxing in Singapore in November 2015 emerged as more style over substance. The image of two rival Chinese state presidents together for the first time since 1949, though certainly historic, nonetheless, raised a number of nervous questions. On the one hand, Xi Jinping appeared to offer his de facto rival a tacit recognition. Yet, Taiwan citizens felt uncomfortable with the political symbolism not to mention to the poignant reality that much of the economic doldrums facing Taiwan can be directly linked to China's slowdown. Equally, the presence of President Xi shadowed the summit.[43]

The 2016 Election

The anxious countdown to Taiwan's 2016 presidential and legislative elections produced far fewer political pyrotechnics than previous contests, reflecting both the island's maturing democracy and an expected pendulum swing from the ruling KMT back to the DPP.

As expected, the opposition won with voters electing Tsai Ing-wen, Taiwan's first female president. The DPP swept back to power with 56 percent of the vote as compared to the fractured KMT team of Eric Chu gaining only 31 percent and James Soong's pro-Unification People First Party getting only 13 percent. Despite Tsai's impressive victory, she fell short of Ma Ying-jeou's 2008 landslide which gained 58 percent of the vote.

But beyond earning the extraordinary symbolism of being the first female president in the Chinese-speaking world, Tsai's DPP surmounted a bigger hurdle; winning the Legislative Yuan, the 113 seat parliament which remained a redoubt of the Nationalists even during the DPP's stormy rule between 2000 and 2008. The KMT lost its 64-seat majority in the parliament. When the dust settled, DPP had won 68 seats compared to the KMT's 35 and the PFP's 3. The upstart New Power Party gained five seats in the legislature.[44]

A scholarly lawyer and trade negotiator with degrees from Cornell University and the London School of Economics, Tsai is more the studied technocrat than the bombastic firebrand.

The dynamics of the election centered on a number of key factors: a downturn in the Taiwan economy, the perception that too close economic ties with the Mainland caused the downturn, and the overall feeling that Taiwan was losing its cherished identity and independence to a raft of deals signed between Ma's administration and Beijing. And, as in the past, the DPP was favored in southern and central parts of the island while the KMT bastions were in the Taipei region.

Middle-class voters, frustrated with tepid economic growth, much of which can be blamed on the over-reliance on the Mainland markets, caused political defections from the KMT. Moreover, poor job prospects and widening social inequality caused a major shift especially among younger and first-time voters who surged to the opposition parties.

Nonetheless, DPP's traditional stance on Taiwan separatism was far less the issue in the 2016 elections than in past contests. While PRC media outlets trumpeted the usual warnings to Taiwan over any hints of "separatism and independence," Beijing exhibited far less political vitriol and threats than in past elections.

Significantly, Tsai Ing-wen has refrained from tinkering with the sensitive rhetorical balance across the Taiwan Strait instead proclaiming a clear and unambiguous commitment to the *status quo*. Indeed, both sides must manage the tenor and tone of rhetoric on such a sensitive issue.

In an interview in the pro-DPP *Liberty Times*, president-elect Tsai stated clearly, "The results of this election demonstrate that maintaining the 'status quo,' which is my policy, is the mainstream view of Taiwanese. Maintaining peace in the Taiwan Strait and the stable development of the cross-strait relationship are the common wish of all groups concerned." She added, "However that responsibility is not unilateral. Both sides must work to build a consistent, predictable and sustainable cross-strait relationship. Maintaining peace in the Taiwan Strait and the stable development of the cross-strait relationship are the common wish of all groups concerned."

Nonetheless, popular pressures could pull her into Taiwan's turbulent political vortex. Tsai stated, "We insist on obeying the democratic will and the democratic principle and we insist on ensuring the freedom of Taiwanese in the right to choose their future. This is the most significant difference between the new administration and the Ma administration."[45]

In her inaugural address in May, President Tsai presented a measured and moderate vision of Taiwan's path ahead. She outlined, "The people elected a new president and a new government with one single expectation: solving problems," and called for Transforming Economic Structures which will reflect the "vibrancy and resilience of a maritime economy," and promotion of a "New Southbound Policy" to diversify the economy and "to bid farewell to our past over reliance on a single market." This was a clear reference to the Mainland trade.

President Tsai equally stressed Regional Peace and Stability and Cross–Strait Relations, she stated notably, "I was elected President of the Republic of China, thus it is my responsibility to safeguard the sovereignty and territory of the Republic of China; regarding problems in the East China Sea and South China Sea, we propose setting aside disputes so as to enable joint development." Importantly, she added that the government would maintain the "existing mechanism for dialogue and communication across the Taiwan Strait (MAC and SEF)." She alluded to the importance of negotiations and interactions since 1992 but equally omitted any specific commitment to the informal "1992 Consensus." Nonetheless, she underscored that the "stable and peaceful development of the cross-strait relationship must be continuously promoted."

Tsai underscored, "The new government will conduct cross-strait affairs in accordance with the Republic of China Constitution ... the two governing parties across the Strait must set aside the baggage of history, and engage in positive dialogue, for the benefit of the people on both sides."

Regarding Diplomatic and Global issues, she added, "We will bring Taiwan closer to the world and the world closer to Taiwan. ... Taiwan has been a model citizen in global civil society." She stressed the island continuing path to wider democracy and what she called "Democracy is a conversation between many diverse values."[46]

On the eve of Tsai's inauguration, the US House of Representatives passed a resolution which underscores longstanding American support for Taiwan. "It is the sense of Congress that the Taiwan Relations Act and the six assurances together form the cornerstone of U.S. relations with Taiwan," the resolution stated. Foreign Affairs Committee Chair Ed Royce (R-CA), "Taiwan has always been a strong friend and a critical ally to the United States. ... It is in the U.S. interest to have a prosperous and stable Taiwan."[47]

President Tsai's address in Taipei before over 1000 government dignitaries and diplomatic allies presented a pragmatic vision which carefully steered clear of both economic populism and anti-China rhetoric; she tread a tactful path.

Regarding Tsai's plan to tilt Taiwan's trade from its Mainland dependence by the New Southward Policy, toward Southeast Asia a skeptical *China Post* editorial questioned, "The idea behind the policy is simple: Don't put all of your eggs in one basket. Yet while there are many baskets, there is no promise that one can actually divide the eggs among them, or that all of the baskets are safe for storing eggs." The editorial added the government must establish mechanisms and programs to help businessmen gain markets in the ASEAN.[48]

Beijing's response to Tsai's inauguration was predictably sullen but muted for the most part.

An editorial in the *China Daily* stated, "Both sides of the Straits need predictability now. Tsai too has said she wants it. ... Her inaugural speech however, was a sign that the relationship may be anything but predictable in the years to come. It left too many crucial questions unanswered. "

The editorial added pedagogically, "Beijing didn't fly into a rage at her ambiguity. But Tsai should finish her answer sheet for the benefits of all people on both sides of the Straits—the earlier the better."[49]

Dr. Jerome Cohen of New York University Law School advised, "If Ms. Tsai fails in her effort to maintain predictable, stable and beneficial cross-strait relations, this will have an undesirable impact on regional security affecting all the neighboring states."⁵⁰

Only time and prudence will manage a complicated Cross–Straits relationship between Taipei and Beijing. Tsai Ing-wen must tread this political tightrope carefully and manage and maintain a *Balance of Peace* across the Taiwan Strait.

Thus, neither the KMT nor the DPP has an exclusive monopoly on ideas in dealing with China.

Managing the *status quo* in the future remains a key challenge for Taiwan's policy makers. For the KMT Nationalists, the link with China's history, culture, and civilization remains a proud political touchstone. The ambitious but reassuring 1992 Consensus, namely that there is but one China albeit with an ambiguous interpretation, offers both sides a working formula within the Chinese context. For the DPP Green camp, avoiding the dangerous ramifications of rhetorical theatrics with China, offers hope for balanced non-confrontation with Beijing and close links with the USA.

Taiwan's political landscape, like its natural surroundings, is surrounded by beautiful blue oceans and lush green mountains and fields, a fitting metaphor for this beautiful island. Both colors in harmony make this island of Formosa such a vibrant and unique place. Yet, Taiwan's cherished sovereignty is largely dependent on a triangular policy of Taipei, Beijing, and Washington. Given political pressures from the PRC rulers, Taiwan has had to rely on a vital but unofficial relationship with the USA for counterbalance. Contrary to South Korea, protected by a defense treaty with the USA, the Taipei government must rely on Washington for favorable policy not clear defense obligations. Balancing the Cross–Strait relationship becomes more complicated given the PRC's politically rigid posture facing Taiwan's prosperous, free, and outspoken Chinese society just 90 miles away.

Notes

1. Full text of President Ma's Inaugural Address/China Post, 21 May 2008, pp. 1–2.
2. Ibid., pp. 1–2.
3. Author Interview, Dr. Shelly Rigger, 1 September 2015.
4. "Taiwan Costa Rica Diplomatic Ties Cut," China Post, 8 June 2007, p. 1 and "Secretive China Agency uses Funds to lure Costa Rica from Taiwan," Financial Times, 12 September 2008, p. 1.

5. Economic Development ROC (Taiwan) Council for Economic Planning and Development/Executive Yuan/Taipei, Taiwan 2010, p. 7.
6. The Development of International Trade in the Republic of China on Taiwan Bureau of Foreign Trade/Ministry of Economic Affairs, Taipei, Taiwan ROC 2009, p. 11.
7. China Post, 6–12 August 2009.
8. Ministry of Foreign Affairs/Republic of China (Taiwan) 21 August 2008 and United Nations General Assembly A/63/194 22 August 2008, pp. 1–4.
9. John J. Metzler, "Rejoining the Club: The Republic of China on Taiwan's Bid for United Nations Participation: Prospects and Portents." presented at the Northeastern Political Science Association, Philadelphia, 17 November 2011, pp. 20–21.
10. Interview at Ministry of Foreign Affairs/ROC Taipei 22 June 2011.
11. Philip Yang, "Taiwan's Smart Strategy for Cross Strait Relations," The Asia Society/New York 12 July 2011, p. 5.
12. Statement by Francisco Alvarez de Soto, Vice Chancellor of Panama, UN General Assembly 22 September 2011, p. 11.
13. Statement by Hon. Ralph Gonsalves, Prime Minister of Saint Vincent and the Grenadines, UN General Assembly 24 September 2011, p. 5.
14. Chiang Pin-kung, New Era in Cross Strait Relations, SEF/Taipei June 2011.
15. "Steering Through a Sea of Change," presented by Ma Ying-jeou, Center on Democracy, Development and the Rule of Law Stanford University 16 April 2013, p. 4 and Author interview Dr. Chiang pin-kung SEF Taipei visit June 2011. The large numbers of cross strait flights is more amazing than the actual number may suggest. Taiwan, a New Hampshire sized island but with twenty three times the population, has nearly 90 flights per day to China.
16. "Chiang Kai-shek's Name Restored to Taipei Monument," China Post, 21 July 2009, p. 1.
17. "ROC Celebrates Centennial year," China Post, 11 October 2011, p. 1.
18. Vincent Wei-cheng Wang Taiwan's 2012 Elections and Taiwan–U.S.–China Relations. April 2012.

19. Full Text of President Ma's Inaugural Address, China Post, 21 May 2012.
20. Chao, Chien-min, "Xi Jinping's Policies Towards Taiwan after the Nine-in-One Elections." Prospect Journal No. 13, Prospect Foundation Taipei, Taiwan, p. 150.
21. Report to Congress; Military and Security Developments Involving the People's Republic of China 2015 (Washington, DC: Secretary of Defense, 2015), pp. 49–50.
22. Ibid., p. 5.
23. Ibid., pp. 57–61.
24. "Ma Panned over 'languishing' military," Taipei Times, 23 June 2011, p. 1.
25. "Pundits say Defense cuts invite aggression," Taipei Times, 22 June 2011, pp. 1, 3.
26. *Military Balance* 2015 IISS London, pp. 237, 287.
27. Ibid., p. 486. A study by the Washington DC based Center for strategic and International Studies (CSIS) revealed that Taiwan's defense spending during the previous decade had risen by a mere 1.8 percent, the lowest level of Asian states such as China, Japan, South Korea or India.
28. Public Opinion on Cross–Strait Relations/Mainland Affairs Council, ROC May 2011.
29. Public Views on Current Cross–Strait Relations/Mainland Affairs Council, ROC July 2014.
30. The Diaoyutai Islands: An Inherent part of the Republic of China (Taiwan), Ministry of Foreign Affairs (Taipei: ROC, 2012).
31. The East China Sea Peace Initiative, Ministry of Foreign Affairs (Taipei: ROC, 2012).
32. "Major Events of Taiwan's Sunflower Movement," China Post, 9 April 2014, p. 1.
33. Op. cit. "Taiwan's Identity Crisis."
34. "Coming attractions; Election Season Hits Taiwan," by Shelly Rigger, E Notes FPRI, June 2015.
35. "Taiwan Election Results 2014; Opposition Wins by a Landslide," U.S./Taiwan Business Council, December 2014, us-taiwan.org.
36. "Taiwan Working to Reduce Trade Reliance on China: Ma," China Post, 10 January 2015, p. 1.
37. Bureau of Foreign Trade/ROC/Taiwan trade.gov.tw. For purposes of China trade, Taiwan combines both PRC and Hong Kong trade numbers.

38. Bush, Richard C., *Uncharted Strait The Future of China-Taiwan Relations*. Washington, DC: Brookings Institution Press, 2013.
39. "Philippine Trade Expands; Trade Value Doubles," China Post, 27 April 2015, p. 1 and Ibid., trade.gov.tw.
40. "China Still #1 Threat, Shen Says," Taipei Times, 22 August 2015, p. 3.
41. "Tsai Vows Stable Ties With Beijing in CSIS Speech," China Post. 5 June 2015, p. 1.
42. "Ma's Ambitious Cross Straits Legacy," Taipei Times, 26 August 2015.
43. "Hands Across the Water," The Economist, 7 November 2015, p. 33.
44. "Madam President," Taipei Times, 17 January 2016, p. 1.
45. "Tsai's Cross Strait Policy to Rest on Democratic Will," Taipei Times, 22 January 2016, p. 1.
46. "President Tsai Ing-wen's Inaugural Address," Taipei Times, 21 May 2016, p. 1.
47. "U.S. Passes Resolution that Outlines Ties with Taiwan," Taipei Times, 18 May 2016.
48. "New Southward Policy Must Entail Concrete Measures," China Post, 21 May 2016.
49. "Tsai's Inaugural Speech Leaves Crucial Straits Questions Unanswered," China Daily, 21 May 2016.
50. "A Stable Transition in Taiwan?" 19 January 2016, CFR.org.

CHAPTER 8

Conclusions: Prospects and Portents

Taiwan stands as an admirable example of a synergy of Confucianism, capitalism, and Chinese entrepreneurialism, which turned a small and war-ravished island into a socio-economic success story and moreover a free-wheeling if occasionally raucous democracy. Few places in East Asia can hold claim to both this economic *and* political success story. Singapore has created an equally amazing socio-economic saga, but its political transformation has remained stagnant. Yet, no place with the exception of South Korea is equally part of a divided nation, still living under the shadow of military confrontation. But, contrary to Seoul, the Taipei government does not have a formal US Defense Treaty offering credible deterrence. Thus, despite the warming of Cross–Strait relations, the issue of security remains paramount for the ROC's ability to defend and preserve its hard won freedom and sovereignty.

In the view of Profs. Inglehart and Welzel, while "modernization is not westernization," they add, "The core idea of modernization theory is that economic and technological development bring a coherent set of social, cultural, and political changes." They add, "Economic development is indeed strongly linked to pervasive shifts in people's beliefs and motivations, and these shifts in turn change the role of religion, job motivation, human fertility rates, gender roles, and sexual norms. And the also bring growing mass demands for democratic institutions and for more responsible behavior on the parts of elites."[1]

Taiwan without question has become a working democracy, largely as the result of high educational standards, sustained economic development, and a society of shared middle-class values.

The ROC on Taiwan has reached a plateau of prosperity and non-marginalization, freedom, and sovereignty. Yet, its survival in a bubble of PRC consensus has never eliminated the political coercion factor from Beijing. Should Taiwan operate out of the confines of a well-established and comfortable *status quo*, the PRC's appetite for such peaceful coexistence may quickly disappear.

Despite many cultural similarities, China and Taiwan are not one. There is a different social and certainly political culture. Linguistic dialects and cuisine differ. And, even the internationally famous Chinese Pandas are not native to Taiwan which boasts its own beloved but equally endangered Formosan Black Bear.

Many scholars speak of *Greater China*, that of vast expanse encompassing the Mainland but specifically coastal China, along with Hong Kong, Taiwan, and Singapore. While there is a thread of common culture and history, the more contact Taiwan has with Mainland the more that genuine democratic concerns arise. Taiwan certainly belongs to a larger *Sinosphere*, but equally proudly holds a unique island identity.

Yet, the 1949 Generation is past on both sides of the Taiwan Strait, and thus the personal animus of the Chinese Civil War is being overcome by the actual blood ties of both sides of the Chinese family. In this sense, generations can move on. The former Sino identity, despite the political chasm across the Strait, has been diluted because of Taiwan's vibrant and often fractious democracy. Moreover, does Taiwan see its future in the context of a Chinese cultural sphere?

Or perhaps one extended Chinese family?

The glue of Han Chinese nationalism binds together the disparate provinces and nationalities on the Mainland much more than the moribund ideological writ of communism.

In its annual survey of human rights, Freedom House offers a comparative analysis of the state of freedoms, political rights, and civil liberties. The scale runs from 1 being perfect to 7 being terrible. Taiwan rates as free with an overall rating of 1.5, rating a 1 in political rights, and 2 in civil liberties. Taiwan ranks ahead all Asia and slightly behind Australia and Japan.

The People's Republic of China, on the other hand, ranks as Not Free with a 6.5 freedom rating, with 7 in political rights, and 6 in civil liberties.

The PRC is surpassed only in tyranny by North Korea and Sudan. Even Burma/Myanmar and Vietnam slightly edge out the PRC's standing.[2]

The Washington-based Heritage Foundation in its 2016 *Index of Economic Freedom* ranks Taiwan number 5 out of 42 Asia-Pacific economies. Using comparative analysis in the fields of Rule of Law, Limited Government, Regulatory Effectiveness, and Open Markets, the overview includes issues like property rights, freedom from corruption, trade freedom, and so on. Out of 178 countries listed, Taiwan ranks as 14 globally, just behind the UK and the USA.

Impressively Hong Kong (Beijing's Special Autonomous Region) ranks number 1.

The People's Republic of China, however, remains in the Most *Unfree* category and ranks as number 144.[3]

As China's economic expansion bought about closer trade with Taiwan, will the PRC's economic woes impact on Taiwan because of precisely such close commercial links? An economically strong and powerful China, while building military muscle, remained far more regionally stable than an economically weaker country whose regime may turn to hyper-nationalism, and military coercion as to presumably right the wrongs and injustices of the past.

Most scenarios presume Taiwan will face an ever stronger PRC regime. But what if an economic slowdown or decline in China causes the PRC to be objectively weaker but, at the same time, more prone to adventurism? Will PRC's stifling authoritarianism combined with its political self-righteousness come to clash with freewheeling Taiwan? Although the lucrative balm of Cross–Strait commerce has soothed over many political contradictions, the fact remains that the PRC appears incapable of compromise with Taiwan.

Richard C. Bush, a former Managing Director of AIT and presently with Brookings, advises that given the PRC's rising military power, "Taiwan could, of course, choose to muddle through by continuing its current three-prong approach: use rhetorical reassurance and greater cross–strait ties to increase Beijing's stake in peace; seek advanced weaponry from the United States in line with its current defense strategy; and maintain defense spending at recent levels, below three percent a year." Yet, Bush adds, "But mudding through would not promote security, because China would likely invest more in military power than Taiwan does. The island's vulnerability to intimidation and pressure would likely increase."[4]

South China Seas Chessboard The idyllic tropical setting of the South China Sea islands can easily overshadow the intense behind-the-scene political maneuvering for sovereignty and status shared among six separate states who lay claim to some or all of the islands scattered throughout the Spratly group.

One of President Ma Ying-jeou's last official trips was a one-day Lunar New Year visit to *Taiping* Island, also known as *Itu Aba*. Ma's journey was all about reinforcing ROC sovereignty in the disputed island group. Taiwan maintains Coast Guard and research facilities on the 110-acre islet, the largest of the Spratly group.

In recent years, the PRC has stoked regional tensions by its claims over the entire South China Sea and has built more than seven artificial islands in the Spratly archipelago. The "nine dash line" has unilaterally marked off China's claim to essentially the entire maritime region. There is an almost James Bondisha James Bond like aura where Chinese engineers are literally constructing islands, airfields, and placing population on otherwise uninhabited shallow shoals. Such moves are seen as a direct affront to both nearby Vietnam and especially the Philippines.

The Spratly region comprises a vast shallow basin holding natural resources and equally serving as a vital sea-lane of communication and trade for all East Asia. The USA has stressed freedom of navigation in the region's international waters. The US Navy has regularly sent vessels through the region to "show the flag" and reinforce the position. Beijing, on the other hand, views the South China Sea as a kind of geopolitical *mare nostrum* much of which it is trying to physically occupy. In fact, Beijing's view of its regional maritime rights may have as much to do with natural resources and military advantage as with national pride and standing.

China, Taiwan, Malaysia, the Philippines, Vietnam, and Brunei have competing claims in the region. In July 2016 a international Tribunal in the Hague rejected and rebuffed many of China's regional maritime claims. The Paracel Islands, *Xisha* in Chinese or *Hoang Sa* in Vietnamese, comprising an archipelago of 130 coral islands and reefs, is equally controlled by Beijing. Known as *Xisha*, the islets were seized from South Vietnam in 1974. Vietnam still claims the islands. China garrisons some of the key islets. The region regularly sees disputes with Vietnamese fishing fleets.

> Source: "Why Taiwan President Ma Ying-jeou's Day Trip to Taiping Island was Such a Big Deal," by Jacques de Lisle FPRI *E Notes* February 2016.

The PRC's power paradigm appears straightforward: supercharged economy/GDP power, Chinese *nationalism* with a self-righteousness of regained status, and a strong military able to both defend borders and project power in regional crises such as the South China Sea. The PRC has mollified its citizens with socio-economic prosperity, has seduced them with high-octane *nationalism, but has kept them in check through the CCP's undisputed one-party rule.*

Would a PRC economic decline cause the leadership to look for nationalistic goals to divert attention? Shall tensions rise in the South China Sea, Taiwan, Daioyutai–Senkaku islands? On a wider scale, would the PRC directly challenge the USA in East Asia?

The Beijing Winter Olympics in 2022 provide a grand opportunity to showcase China but, at the same time, offer Taiwan a "security valve" as the image conscious PRC leadership does not want a political standoff with the island democracy to spoil the party. Having hosted the 2008 Summer Olympiad and the Winter Olympics will make the Chinese capital the first city to hold this double distinction.

Equally, it is imperative that the Taipei government maintain close relations with Washington, as, in the opinion of Richard Bush, "to strengthen U.S. confidence that Taiwan will not act in ways that are inconsistent with the American interest in peace and stability in the Taiwan Strait. U.S. confidence was undermined during the Lee Teng-hui and Chen Shui-bian administrations but strengthened under Ma Ying-jeou." He adds, "Taiwan's challenge is to create the impression in Beijing's mind that it has the confidence to stand up to the implied military threat embodied in a Chinese pressure campaign because it has the ability to survive a PLA attack on its own for as long as the United States takes to decide whether to intervene."[5]

An interesting seldom mentioned variable regarding US ties to Taiwan and interest in the larger China issue concerns the actual image and knowledge of Taiwan in the minds of the American public. While Taiwan generally is well known and respected, the deeper personal knowledge and identification that Americans have is largely based on the island's thriving economy and possibly its democratic political system. Nonetheless, the close ideological sentiments which even average Americans held for "Free China" during the Cold War era, especially when it was opposing an equally radicalized communist China, is simply not the same. Thus, while Americans "of a certain generation" still admire Taiwan, most younger people know little of the island beyond its economic prowess. One could assume that many Americans supported Taiwan as a reflection of their fears and dislike for the once revolutionary regime in the People's Republic of China.

Equally, the views of China have vastly changed from the political prism of the proletarian and radical Maoist era, to the evolving image of an economically reformist China as "factory to the world," a serious trade competitor, but increasingly now as a military competitor. Beijing nonetheless views Taiwan's status as a "domestic issue."

According to a *Pew Poll*, "Nearly two-thirds describe relations between the U.S. and China as good, and most consider China a competitor rather than an enemy." Yet, when viewing the specifics, the report adds,

> "Just 10% of Americans say they have heard a lot about relations between China and Taiwan; 54% have heard a little, and 34% have heard nothing at all about the issue ... about half (48%) of those who have heard a lot about relations between China and Taiwan say the U.S. should use military force to defend Taiwan if China were to use force against the island; 43% say the U.S. should not use military force to defend Taiwan."

Significantly, the report adds that the presumed use of US military force depends on the circumstances; majorities of five expert groups (government, retired military, business, news media, and scholars) would support the use of US military force to defend Taiwan if China moved against the island without a unilateral declaration of independence by Taiwan.[6] Stated another way, Taiwan's support in the USA remains solid *provided* the Taipei government does not deliberately provoke the PRC with separatist actions.

Scenarios

Logical Rapprochement? While both the Mainland and Taiwan have come closer together on the socio-economic scale, there is little official political rapprochement to suggest that the CCP can come to terms with a democratic Taiwan. Stressing values integration such as more Cross–Straits travel and tourism, already reaching impressive numbers in both directions, is one such step. So too are students who respectively study "on the other side of the Strait." Yes to a point, this will lower social barriers, but shall it bring about calls for the grand national bargain of Chinese reunification?

Status Quo? Most Taiwanese will not risk their hard won prosperity and lifestyle for the lure of rhetoric and an almost certain showdown with PRC regime. Thus, most public opinion polls overwhelmingly support the *status quo*. Maintaining the *status quo* moreover depends in some part on American weapons' sales so that Taiwan's defenses and deterrence remain credible in the face of a quantitative and increasingly qualitative PRC military force modernization. Taiwan needs to maintain air superiority and American F-16 C and D sales and upgrades remain an absolute minimum. So too should be an enhancement of Taiwan's diesel submarine capacity, anti-submarine warfare, and minesweeper capacity as to counter and PRC's moves toward blockade or sea-lane interdiction. In other words, *the* status quo *is not just a state of mind, or a state of inaction, but a step toward active deterrence.*

Separatism/Independence This possibility has long been the lightning rod for a PRC attack. What can/would the USA do? Though many pundits point to the Taiwan Relations Act (TRA) enacted in 1979 as a way to safeguard Taiwan's status, the act is not a Mutual Defense Treaty. *While the TRA outlines policy, it does not give the USA a* de jure *obligation to defend the ROC.* The PRC has never renounced the use of force to bring Taiwan "back to the motherland." Thus, any moves incremental or sudden to declare "independence" or to rhetorically tinker with the national constitution, symbols, and formal *de jure* name of the Republic of China could trigger a response by Beijing. China's 2005 "Anti-Secession Law" is part of a long list of Beijing's dire warnings to Taiwan independence. For all practical purposes, Taiwan is a de facto state; any political party advocating separatism is playing with fire. For any government in Taipei to assume that the TRA offers the security of a formal defense treaty would equally be in error. The DPP government is challenged to tread carefully in the rhetorical minefield in defining Taiwan's status while at the same time responding to the democratic wishes of the electorate.

PRC Invasion/US Response The Beijing rulers have never renounced the use of military force to bring Taiwan "back to the Motherland," or "teach the island a lesson." Happily, this outcome has never come to pass despite some harrowing experiences, especially during Taiwan's presidential elections in 1996, when the PRC lobbed some missiles into the waters

around the island. The USA resounded swiftly and decisively with the dispatch of a US Navy Carrier battle group, which quickly calmed the PRC's appetite for conflict. Now, 20 years later, and facing both a much larger and qualitative PRC military, and with a smaller US Navy, does the USA have the political will and military capacity to engage in such a risky operation? Despite the Obama administration's much heralded "Pacific Pivot," namely the strategic re-balance of American attention toward the Pacific, the actual U.S. military resources allocated toward the region have not been sufficient to reduce regional fears and concerns over the PRC's growing geopolitical focus toward disputed islands with Japan, contested waters and islets in the South China Sea, and, of course, Taiwan.
The TRA asserts that

> "efforts to determine the future of Taiwan by other than peaceful means, including by boycotts or embargoes, would be a threat to the peace and security of the Western Pacific and of grave concern to the United States ... the President and Congress shall determine, in accordance with the constitutional processes, appropriate action by the United States in response to any such danger."

In the opinion of Dr. Ted Galen Carpenter, "Such vague provisions are a far cry from a defense obligation, even an implied one." He adds, "If Congress had intended to incorporate the provisions of the mutual defense treaty into the TRA, it could have done so. But it explicitly rejected an amendment that would have incorporated the previous obligations." As Carpenter adds, "The problem with the TRA is that it can be interpreted in a multitude of ways ... over the decades, a succession of U.S. administrations have pursued a de facto policy of strategic ambiguity, at times deliberately, to keep both Taipei and Beijing guessing about what the United States would actually do in response to a military crisis in the Taiwan Strait."[7]

Finlandization Taiwan's democratic system, unwieldy as it may be, nonetheless confronts the PRC's authoritarian political structure with profound political uncertainties. Thus, the PRC has confronted the island with a number of seemingly generous deals, such as "one country, two systems," to try to peacefully lure Taiwan back into the fold. China's sugarcoated political offers are viewed with suspicion. Thus, Beijing is focusing on economic invectives to engage Taiwan. Even media has been influenced by Beijing's "soft power" projection. In Taiwan, many media owners have close commercial ties to China and thus depend on advertising and are often prone to self-censorship.

During the Cold War, the term *Finlandization* evoked a process where one powerful country (Soviet Union) influences the policies of a smaller neighboring state (Finland) but still allowing the weaker land to maintain its independence and political system. The Finlandization process referred to predominant Soviet influence over neighboring Finland's policies. Thus *Finlandization*. Given the close commercial relations across the Taiwan Strait, never mind the national and ethnic similarity (certainly not the case with Finland), Taiwan's fears of *Finlandization* from looming Mainland economic links and political shadows have increased. In other words, Taiwan's political flexibility could be compromised by close commercial dependence on China. As a counterweight to China's economic magnetism, Taipei would be wise to deepen its trade with traditional partners such as the USA, Japan, and the ASEAN countries and seek new markets in India and Latin America.

Richard Bush opines,

> "A serious effort by Taiwan to strengthen its sense of sovereignty, economic competitiveness, security, political system, and U.S. relationship will not guarantee a completely satisfactory outcome with China. What is certain is that refusal to engage in self-strengthening or failure to do it well, will give Beijing significant advantages in how it deals with Taiwan, whether through mutual persuasion or exploiting power asymmetry, and how its fundamental dispute with the island's government is ultimately resolved."[8]

Firm and focused American support to the island democracy remains vital, especially with the change of government in Taipei from the long-ruling KMT to the separatist-inclined DPP. "Given its location at a strategic crossroad of the Asia-Pacific, Taiwan will remain an indispensable part of the U.S. regional security architecture," asserts an article "Rebalancing Taiwan–US Relations," in the journal *Survival*. "U.S. regional allies and partners, such as Japan, South Korea and Southeast Asian countries, thus also have much at stake in Washington's continuing commitment to Taiwan. Cutting Taiwan loose will not only weaken U.S. credibility as a reliable partner, but will also enhance the PRC's ability to project power, should the island fall into its orbit." The article adds, "The fate of Taiwan's autonomy is a litmus test of China's wider intentions as well as U.S. resolution and commitment to the Asia-Pacific."[9]

The Roads Ahead?

So, how shall Taiwan safely secure its sovereignty and freedom in the shadow of China?

In the 1990s, *Sinologists* spoke of a Greater China, a formula of sorts comprising Mainland China, Hong Kong, Taiwan, and usually Singapore. Professor Harry Harding, in an article in *China Quarterly*, viewed a concept with three themes: economic integration, cultural interaction, and eventual political reunification. While Greater China was once part of a trendy vocabulary of international relations such as New World Order, the End of History and Clash of Civilizations, and Pacific Century, the term Greater China asserts Harding "is a controversial concept."

Others have spoken about a Chinese Commonwealth or Confederation, equally a system of shared culture, language, and values but with loose political control. The term *Sinosphere* refers to the cultural and linguistic links among Chinese-speaking states but does not address the core issue of political control.

Plainly stated, would a CCP regime be willing to share or defuse its power and control and allow for regional formulae among the Greater China states? In Hong Kong's case, the CCP has played its cards carefully in the years since the British handover in 1997 to use the phrase, the Chinese communists "have not killed Hong Kong's economic golden goose," and realistically the Special Administrative Region (SAR) has truly prospered. Politically, and especially in the realm of media rights, the PRC has slowly begun to suffocate Hong Kong's once vibrant and feisty press.

The core of CCP Chairman's Xi Jinping's ideology is the "Chinese dream." According to Dr. Chao Chien-min, "elements can be extracted from this ideology in Cross–Strait affairs: Racial restoration, whole interests of the nation and the Chinese race, patriotism, unity and unification, shared growth, and peaceful development."

He adds,

> "Among the six, the first three are the most frequently cited. In a nutshell, nationalism lies at the center of Xi's thinking toward Taiwan. Examining the speeches he made in meetings with Taiwanese leaders, including Vincent Siew, Wu Po-hsiung, Lien Chan, and James Soong, collected in Xi Jinping *Talks about Governing the Country*, the 'whole interests of the Chinese race,' the 'great restoration of the Chinese race,' and the 'beautiful future' are the most cited. Xi is a highly nationalistic leader, and his policies will no doubt reflect upon this temperament."[10]

In early September 2015, China commemorated 70th anniversary of the victory over Japan in WWII. A massive military parade in Beijing set the stage not merely for the remembrances of China's long and bloody struggle against Imperial Japan but for other contemporary lessons as well to remind neighboring states Vietnam, Philippines, Taiwan, and of course Japan that People's Republic of China is a potent military power, to underscore PRC power vis-à-vis territorial disputes such as the Diaoyutai–Senkaku Islands, to assert China's regional role in spite of America's "Pacific Pivot," and perhaps most of all to legitimize the political leadership of President/CCP Chairman Xi Jinping.

The synthesis of Beijing's show of force was the message that the PRC under the leadership of Xi and the CCP stands as a powerful international player. Possibly so.

Yet, a politically brittle PRC state which must constantly remind the world *and* itself that it has emerged as a superpower can be a very unpredictable stakeholder in the Pacific.

The hyper-nationalism which characterizes Xi Jinping's rule seems destined to clash with Taiwan's perceptions of "international space" and the island's effective de facto sovereignty. Economic weakness on the Mainland moreover may encourage the Beijing leadership to play a tougher political game with Taiwan as to revive regime support through nationalist sentiments.

Such a political reality confronts all the colors of Taiwan's political rainbow. The *Pan Blue* KMT stalwarts while wanting closer cultural and economic ties to the Mainland may find themselves caught in a rip current in the Taiwan Strait, which may pull them closer to political accommodation with Beijing's wishes. The *Pan Green* DPP parties face a double dilemma: balancing Taiwan's domestic desires for more *Taiwanization* and correspondingly less *Chineseness* of the social and political space, while at the same time, not allowing separatist rhetoric to reach levels which will certainly provoke a PRC military reaction. It appears that the current DPP leaders have the temperament to manage relations rather than probing and testing Beijing's patience and reactions.

The PRC's rulers, while flexible on the economic front, are likely incapable of serious political change or compromise, either domestically or in ties with Taiwan. Both Taiwan's Blue/Green political spectrum is well aware of China's political atrophy and remains decidedly nervous to come to any closer to willful *rapprochement* with Beijing's rulers. At the same time, unforeseen events in China may offer surprising possibilities and options for all sides.

In past decades, geopolitical realities focused on maintaining a precarious *Balance of Power* across the Taiwan Strait between the PRC and the ROC. Recent years have witnessed a meltdown in the political animosity which once characterized Beijing–Taipei relations. Taipei's government must redouble its efforts to maintain a *Balance of Peace* across the Taiwan Straits.

Notes

1. Op. cit., How Development Leads to Democracy.
2. Freedom House, 2016 Freedom in the World, freedomhouse.org
3. Heritage Foundation, 2016 Index of Economic Freedom, heritage.org
4. Bush, Richard C. *Uncharted Strait: The Future of China-Taiwan Relations.* Washington, DC: Brookings Institution Press, 2013.
5. Ibid. p. 176.
6. PEW Research Center Poll, September 18, 2012.
7. Op. cit., *America's Coming War with China*, pp. 122–123.
8. Op. cit., *Uncharted Strait*, p. 195.
9. "Rebalancing Taiwan-US Relations." Nien-chung Chang Liao and Dalton Kuen-da Lin. *Survival*, Vol. 57, No. 6, December 2015–January 2016, p. 147.
10. "Xi Jinping's Policies towards Taiwan." Chien-min Chao, *Prospect Journal*/Taiwan Forum, April 2015, No. 13, pp. 146–147.

ANNEX

Contents

Maps and Photographs	150
Taiwan's Modernization Matrix	154
Taiwan Diplomatic Recognition as of January 2016	155
Religion in Taiwan	157
Terms, Names, Places	158
Economic Growth and Mainland Chinese Visitors to Taiwan	160
Taiwan Media: An Overview	161
Taiwan's Unsung Foreign Assistance Program	164
Cross-Straits Interactions Between Taiwan and PRC	165

© The Editor(s) (if applicable) and The Author(s) 2017
J.J. Metzler, *Taiwan's Transformation*,
DOI 10.1057/978-1-137-56442-9

Maps and Photographs

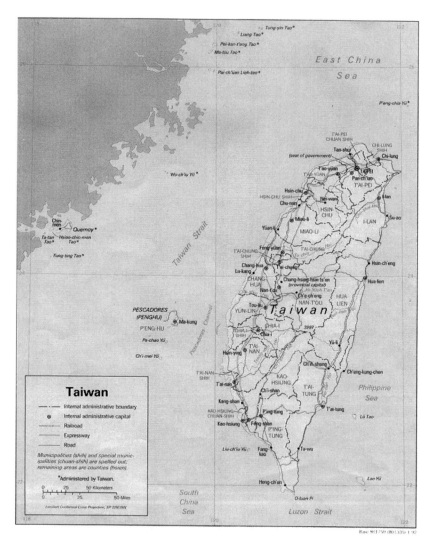

Map 1 Taiwan. Source: University of Texas, Perry-Castañeda Library

ANNEX 151

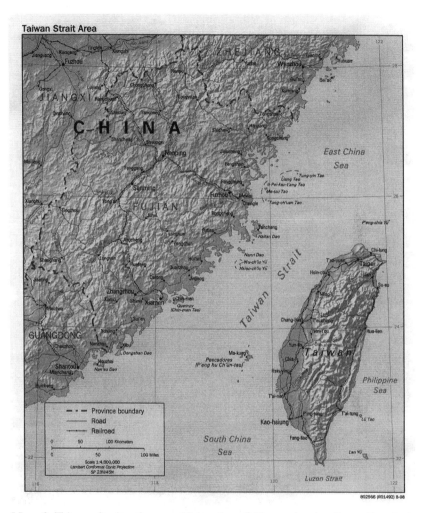

Map 2 Taiwan Straits. Source: University of Texas, Austin, Perry-Castañeda Library

Photo 1 Kaohsiung city and harbor. The southern city of Kaohsiung remains Taiwan major port city and is in fact one of Asia's largest container ports

Photo 2 Downtown Taipei traffic. Taiwan's society has evolved from motorbikes to cars in recent decades. Taipei has become an increasingly "green" and "wired" city

Photo 3 Taiwan Old and New. Reflection from a temple on the glass of a modern building

154 ANNEX

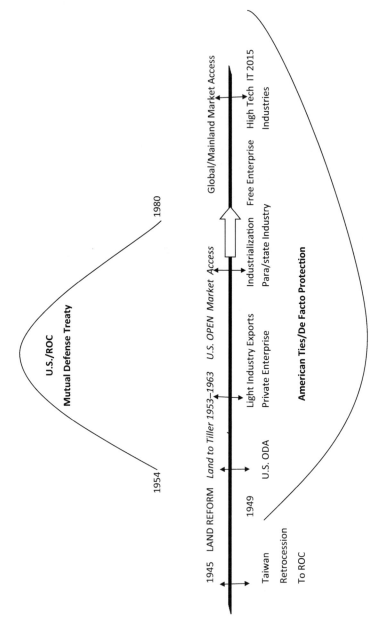

Taiwan Diplomatic Recognition as of January 2016

Table A1 Countries with which the ROC/Taiwan maintains full diplomatic relations: 22

Asia/Pacific

Kiribati	Republic of the Marshall Islands
Nauru	Republic of Palau
Solomon Islands	Tuvalu

Africa

Burkina Faso	Republic of São Tomé and Principe
Kingdom of Swaziland	

Europe

Holy See/Vatican

Latin America/Caribbean

Belize	Dominican Republic
El Salvador	Republic of Guatemala
Haiti	Republic of Honduras
Nicaragua	Republic of Panama
Paraguay	Federation of St. Christopher and Nevis
St. Lucia	St. Vincent and the Grenadines

Source: ROC/Taiwan Ministry of Foreign Affairs, Taipei.

Table A2 Taiwan de facto overseas representation (select examples)

Asia/Pacific
Taipei Economic and Cultural Office in Australia
Taipei Economic and Trade Office, Jakarta, Indonesia
Taipei Economic and Cultural Representative Office in Japan
Taipei Mission in Korea
Taipei Representative Office in Singapore
Taipei Economic and Cultural Office Hanoi, Vietnam

Africa
Taipei Liaison Office in the RSA
Trade Mission of the ROC (Taiwan) Abuja, Federal Republic of Nigeria

Europe
Taipei Economic and Cultural Office, Vienna Austria
Taipei Representative Office in France
Taipei Representative Office in the Federal Republic of Germany
Taipei Representative Office Budapest, Hungary
Taipei Representative Office, Bratislava
Taipei Mission in Sweden
Taipei Representative Office in the U.K.

(continued)

Table A2 (continued)

North America
Taipei Economic and Cultural Office in Canada
Ottawa, Toronto and Vancouver
Taipei Economic and Cultural Office Representative Office in the U.S. (TECO)
Washington, DC, Atlanta, Boston, Chicago, Denver, Guam, Honolulu, Houston, Los Angeles, Miami, New York, San Francisco, Seattle.

Latin America
Taipei Commercial and Cultural office in Argentina
Taipei Economic and Cultural Office in Chile
Commercial Office of the Republic of China (Taiwan) in Ecuador
Taipei Economic and Cultural Office in Mexico

Religion in Taiwan

Once while visiting Tamkang University in Taipei for a lecture, I was amazed to see the school next to an impressive, if improbable, Mormon temple. And right across the street stood the Apostolic Nuncio of the Holy See, the diplomatic delegation of the Vatican. The Grand Mosque is nearby as is the Holy Family Catholic Church.

While there is freedom of religion in Taiwan, there equally seems to be a proliferation of religions on the island from the majority Buddhism with followers about 35% of the population and Taoism with followers numbering 33%.

Yet about 80% of people on the island follow "folk religions," which also may overlap with the more mainstream Asian faiths. Temples and local deities proliferate.

Included among some of the folk faiths are the Yi Guan Dao, Heaven Emperor Religion, Heaven Virtue Religion, Yellow Emperor Religion, and Yellow Middle Religion. The goddess of Matsu is particularly revered by fishermen and seafarers.

Christian faiths proliferate but form a small segment of the overall population: Protestant groups include Presbyterians, Baptists, and Lutherans.

The Roman Catholic Church comprises about two percent of the population. Yet there are seven Catholic Dioceses on the island and the church runs the Fu Jen Catholic University. Though the Vatican and the ROC have maintained diplomatic ties since 1942, the Holy See has expressed a desire to open ties with Beijing, providing the Chinese government permits true freedom of religion and drops a number of onerous restrictions on the faith.

Interestingly most of the indigenous peoples in Taiwan are either Protestant or Catholic.

Many if not most of the Christians equally follow the Confucian ethical path.

Most of the 200,000 Indonesian migrant workers are Muslim while the Filipinos are Christian.

According to a report of the American Institute in Taiwan (AIT), "The constitution and other laws and policies protect religious freedom and, in practice, the authorities generally respected religious freedom."

The document adds: "There were no reports of societal abuses or discrimination based on religious affiliation, belief, or practice."

Source: American Institute in Taiwan (AIT) International Religious Freedom Report and *Religion in Modern Taiwan: Tradition and Innovation in a Changing Society*, Philip Clart, Editor, Honolulu: University of Hawaii Press, 2003.

Terms, Names, Places

Treaties and Agreements

Treaty of Shimonoseki, 1895: Ends the First Sino-Japanese War but cedes Formosa to Japan.

Cairo Conference, 1943: Allied pledge to restore Formosa to the ROC after WWII ends.

Mutual Defense Treaty, 1954: US-ROC defense treaty crafted by John Foster Dulles.

Shanghai Communiqué, 1972: During the Nixon visit to China, the USA and PRC agree there is "one China" with different interpretations.

Taiwan Relations Act (TRA), 1979: Bi-partisan Congressional support package in the wake of Carter administration diplomatic recognition of Beijing in 1979.

1992 Consensus: Informal agreement between PRC and Taiwan that there is "one China" but with different interpretations.

Key Dates and Terms

Taiwan Retrocession, 1945: Japan surrenders its colony to the ROC after WWII ends.

The tragic February 28, 1947 incident was sparked over the selling of allegedly contraband cigarettes. Government officers assaulted, a 40-year-old widow selling cigarettes in Taipei. The incident soon turned into a confrontation between the officials and angry onlookers. Violence spread like wildfire throughout Taipei and Keelung, with attacks on Mainlanders and government property. Martial law was imposed.

Land to the Tiller: Land Reform Movement which distributed land to farmers and boosted private ownership, morale, and food production starting in the 1950s.

Ten Major Construction Projects: Infrastructural projects started in the 1970s, building freeways, ports, steel mills, shipyards, etc. as a way to jumpstart economic growth.

Key Political Names

Chiang Kai-shek: Nationalist China's wartime leader, President of the ROC until his death in 1975.

Chiang Ching-kuo: Chiang's son and ROC president between 1975; lifted martial law in 1987 and allowed for cautious democratization. He died in 1988.

Lee Teng-hui: A native Taiwanese KMT figure elected president in 1996.

Chen Shui-bian: Two-term DPP-separatist-inclined president elected in 2000 and in 2004.

Ma Ying-jeou: Two-term KMT status quo inclined president elected in 2008 and reelected in 2012.

Political Parties

KMT—Kuomintang or Nationalist Party: Pro-unification under democracy and rooted in Taiwan's Chinese heritage and status quo. Party of government on Taiwan, from 1945 until 2000–2008. Regained the presidency in 2008–2016.

DPP—Democratic Progressive Party: An opposition *tangwai* party strongly rooted in Taiwan identity and often political separatism away from the "one China" theory. DPP is strong in southern Taiwan and increasingly on the local level. Party of government between 2000 and 2008.

PFP—People First Party: Established in 2000 as a breakaway from the KMT. Conservative, pro-reunification, and against separatism, the PFP is part of the pan-Blue alignment. The party has fared poorly in recent years at the national and local level.

TSU—Taiwan Solidarity Union: Founded in 2001 by as a party with the clear aim of Taiwan independence. Part of the pan-Green coalition, the TSU holds a few seats on the national level.

Pan-Blue: Represents the KMT Blue and smaller parties aligned with unification.

Pan-Green: Represents the DPP and smaller parties aligned with a Taiwanese vision and sometimes political separatism.

Agencies

MAC—Mainland Affairs Council: A cabinet-level administrative agency tasked to formulate and facilitate social and economic interchanges with Mainland China.

MAC carries out high-level talks with its Mainland Chinese counterparts. Equally, MAC publishes periodic opinion polls to take the pulse of cross-straits relations.

SEF—*Straits Exchange Foundation*: A semi-official group established in 1991 and tasked to handle economic and social contacts that would be described as unofficial consular relations with Taiwan citizens living in or dealing with Mainland China. SEF's role has been an unofficial facilitator in contacts with China.

Economic Growth and Mainland Chinese Visitors to Taiwan

Table A3 Taiwan economic growth rates and per capita incomes (select years)

Year	Economic growth rate	Per capita income
1991	8.36%	$9136
1995	6.5%	$13,129
2000	6.4%	$14,941
2005	5.4%	$16,500
2010	10.6%	$19,278
2011	3.8%	$21,000
2012	2.06%	$21,308
2013	2.2%	$21,902
2014	3.7%	$22,635
2015	1.56% (F)	$22,704

Source: National Statistics/Republic of China (Taiwan), eng.stat.gov.tw

(F): Forecast

Table A4 Mainland Chinese visitors to Taiwan (select monthly statistics)

Year	January	July
2001	18,217	17,984
2003	20,391	17,386
2005	12,200	18,255
2009	43,995	70,157
2010	86,891	129,160
2011	101,354	135,968
2012	140,423	235,447
2013	195,388	248,683
2014	268,861	343,709
2015	321,458	352,625

Source: National Statistics/Republic of China (Taiwan), eng.stat.gov.tw

Taiwan Media: An Overview

"The media environment in Taiwan is among the freest in Asia, and extremely competitive," according to a BBC assessment. Indeed, there is a plethora of viewpoints found in a free press and fiercely independent media in general. And cable TV outlets provide for a near free-for-all when it comes to topics and opinions.

It was not always that way. In Taiwan's earlier years, newspapers were few and towed the KMT political line; censorship on print and audio media was pretty tough, and independent media was rare or harassed. By the 1980s, as the island experienced wider socio-economic prosperity, ensuing political changes were soon felt in the media. For example, in the early years, newspaper size even of the official outlets was a mere eight pages. However, by the 1980s, the size had expanded to 12 pages. When formal press restrictions ended in 1988, papers expanded to 32 or 40 pages. The number of newspapers jumped from 31 in 1987 at the end of martial law to 360 by 1998.

A few major newspapers are listed:

United Daily News: Chinese-language daily, KMT pan-Blue orientation.
China Times: Chinese-language daily, pan-Blue.
Liberty Times: Chinese-language daily, pan-Green orientation.
The China Post: English-language daily, pan-Blue orientation.
The Taipei Times: English-language daily, DPP orientation.

Major broadcast TV outlets are listed:

China Television Company (CTV).
Chinese Television System (CTS).
Taiwan Television Enterprise (TTV).
Formosa Television (FTV): affiliated with the DPP.
Public Television Service (PTS): non-profit public broadcaster.

Besides the regular broadcast stations, there is an expanding cable TV market with wide viewership and freewheeling opinions. Interestingly, Mainland Chinese tourists visiting Taiwan, often cite one of the favorite activities is watching Taiwan TV programs, where spontaneous ideas and free opinions provide a fresh alternative to what they are used to back home in China.

Some radio outlets are listed too:

Broadcasting Corporation of China (BCC): national and regional networks.
Radio Taiwan International: broadcasts to Mainland China and overseas in Chinese dialects and foreign languages.
International Community Radio Taipei (ICRT): English language FM; once part of the US Armed Forces Radio, this facility was due to be shut down when Washington terminated ties with Taipei. The American Chamber of Commerce and businessmen came together to turn the facility into a station for the island's international community which it has since served.

The respected human rights monitor *Freedom House* reports, "Taiwan's media reflect a diversity of views and report aggressively on government policies and corruption allegations, though many outlets display strong party affiliation in their coverage." Interestingly the human rights monitor adds, "Beijing has exerted growing influence on Taiwanese media. A number of media owners have significant business interests in China or rely on advertising by Chinese companies, leaving them vulnerable to pressure and prone to self-censorship on topics considered sensitive by the Chinese government. Pro-Beijing advertisements disguised as news are often placed in the Taiwanese media."

Freedom House adds, "The government refrains from restricting the internet."

The French media monitor *Reporters Without Borders* lists Taiwan's media as the freest in the Far East and ahead of Japan, South Korea, and Hong Kong. Mainland China's media ranks 176 out of 180 comparators.

While media outlets have long been divided between KMT/Pan Blue and DPP/Pan Green ideologies, the growing danger according to journalists is that media owners on both sides are undermining the country's freewheeling press in order to protect their expanding business interests on Mainland China. According to a report of the New York–based *Committee to Protect Journalists*, "Broadcast outlets in particular have come under fire recently as pro-China tycoons have sought to monopolize the airwaves."

"Like in Hong Kong, the tycoon bosses of Taiwan media are increasingly pushing their media companies to flatter Beijing because they do business with China," said Chen Hsiao-yi, chairwoman of the Association of Taiwan Journalists and a longtime *Liberty Times* reporter.

"Taiwan media are becoming more and more reliant on Chinese advertising. They are self-censoring for mostly financial and not political reasons," she added.

Sources: Asia/Taiwan Profile Media, bbc.com; Freedom House/Country List Taiwan file, http://freedomhouse.org; Reporters Without Borders/Country List, http://rsf.org; *Republic of China Yearbook/1999*, pp. 275, 282–285; *Attacks on the Press/Journalism on the World's Front Lines 2014*, p. 85.

Taiwan's Unsung Foreign Assistance Program

Since 1959, the ROC government has been providing agricultural assistance and technical aid to foreign countries. Starting first in South Vietnam and later expanding to a number of Taipei's African allies, various agricultural self-help programs have become a hallmark of Taiwan's foreign aid or Overseas Development Assistance (ODA).

Contrary to the often-massive prestige projects many countries engage in throughout the developing world, Taiwan's programs are focused on small and sustainable agriculture, fishing, and microcredit loans. I recall chancing upon one such project in rural Panama in the 1980s where Taiwan agricultural technical experts had set up a watermelon farm to help a local community find exportable produce.

In 1996, the government formalized operations under the International Cooperation and Development Fund (ICDF), a group which now has a quiet but noteworthy presence in more than 20 developing countries from Africa to Central America, the Caribbean, and the South Pacific. Projects cover a wide range from housing reconstruction in El Salvador, Honduras, and Nicaragua to a safe water treatment plant in Haiti, technical education in the Gambia and Guatemala, and microcredit projects in St. Vincent and the Grenadines and St. Kitts and Nevis. And there are tourism and highway repair in Belize and farm irrigation in Swaziland.

There are medical care missions in Burkina Faso, Malawi, and São Tomé.

The point is that these projects, while low key and out of the headlines, make a major difference in needy societies. Beyond stressing agricultural skills, the ICDF also focuses on environmental protection, public health, and information technology.

Presently there are 159 staffers working in 32 missions in 28 partner countries.

Currently the ODA comprises only 0.09% of Taiwan GDP, or approximately $366 million in 2013; a relatively small sum given Taiwan's development.

Taiwan technical assistance is notably focused on its 22 political allies but is still sent to a number of countries which no longer have diplomatic ties with Taipei such as the Gambia, Indonesia, Jordan, and South Africa.

In addition to ODA, Taiwan has played a yeoman role in offering humanitarian assistance in a number of natural disasters such as the Haitian earthquake in 2010 by sending $18.5 million in aid. Equally, Taiwan dispatched emergency assistance to the Philippines using naval vessels and aircraft following Typhoon Haiyan in 2013.

Source: International Cooperation and Development Fund, ICDF. org.tw

Cross-Straits Interactions Between Taiwan and PRC

Table A5 China/Taiwan contact chart form 1955 to 2016

	1955	1975	2000	2015
Political basket				
Cross-recognition	No	No	No	No
Permanent representatives	No	No	No	No
High-level contacts	No	No	Flux	Flux
United nations membership	Yes ROC	Yes PRC	Yes PRC	Yes PRC
Economic basket				
Trade ties	No	No	Yes*	Yes
Cross-investments	No	No	Yes*	Yes*
Direct air transport	No	No	Flux	Yes
Bank loans	No	No	No	Flux
Security basket				
Foreign defense treaty	Yes	Yes	No	No
Foreign troop presence	Yes	Yes	No	No
Nuclear weapons	No	Yes PRC	Yes PRC	Yes PRC
Non-aggression pact	No	No	No	No
Socio-humanitarian basket				
Telephone links	No	No	Yes*	Yes*
Postal links	No	Yes*	Yes*	Yes*
Monetary convertibility	No	No	Yes*	Yes*
Family/Tourist visits	No	No	Yes*	Yes*

This table reflects shared links between both sides of the Taiwan Straits in the *Political, Economic, Security*, and *Social* sectors

Yes* connotes a *de facto* but *unofficial* relationship, such as Taiwan's former trade to Mainland China via Hong Kong

Bibliography

Government Documents & Official Sources

Department of Defense. *The United States Security Strategy for the East Asian-Pacific Region.* Washington, DC: Office of International Security Affairs, 1998.
_____. Annual Report to Congress. *Military Power of the People's Republic of China 2008.*
_____. Annual Report to Congress. *Military and Security Developments Involving the People's Republic of China 2015.*
Development of International Trade in the Republic of China (Taiwan), 2010–2011. Taipei: Ministry of Economic Affairs, 2011.
Economic Development in the Republic of China. Taipei, ROC: Ministry of Economic Affairs, 1975.
Economic Development ROC (Taiwan). Council for Economic Planning and Development/Executive Yuan, Taipei: Council for Economic Planning, 2010.
Jacoby, Neil. *An Evaluation of U.S. Economic Aid to Free China 1951–1965.* Washington, DC: Agency for International Development/Bureau of Far East Aid, 1966.
Japan Yearbook 1935. Tokyo: The Foreign Affairs Association of Japan, 1935.
Ma, Ying-jeou. *Steering Through a Sea of Change.* Center on Democracy, Development and the Rule of Law, Stanford University (video conference) 16 April 2013.
Republic of China Yearbook: 1972–1973, 1977, 1994, 1999. Taipei: China Publishing.
United Nations *Bulletin.*
_____. *Economic and Social Survey of Asia and the Pacific 2014.* Bangkok: ESCAP/United Nations, 2014.

_____. *Economic and Social Survey of Asia and the Pacific 2015*/Part 1. Bangkok: ESCAP/United Nations, 2015.
_____. General Assembly; Official Documents.
_____. Security Council; Official Documents.
_____. *World Investment Report 2015*. New York: United Nations, 2015.
_____. *Yearbook of the United Nations:* 1961–1971.
U.S. Department of State. *American Foreign Policy 1950–1955*; Basic Documents. Washington, DC: GPO, 1957.
_____. *Foreign Relations of the United States* (FRUS). Washington, DC: GPO.
_____. *Memorandums, Telegrams, and Correspondence.* Formosa File 1950s. Washington, DC: National Archives.
_____. *United States Relations with China/with Special Reference to the Period 1944–1949*. Far Eastern series #30. Washington, DC, 1949.

Books

Attacks on the Press; Journalism on the World's Front Lines 2014. New York: Committee to Protect Journalists, 2014.
Bachrack, Stanley D. *The Committee of One Million; "China Lobby" Politics 1953–1971.* New York: Columbia University Press, 1976.
Bernstein, Richard and Ross Munro. *The Coming Conflict with China.* New York: Random House, 1998.
Bush, Richard C. *Uncharted Straits: The Future of China-Taiwan Relations.* Washington, DC: Brookings Institution Press, 2013.
Butterfield, Fox. *China Alive in the Bitter Sea.* New York: Times Books, 1982.
Carpenter, Ted Galen. *America's Coming War with China; A Collision Course over Taiwan.* New York: Palgrave Macmillan, 2005.
Chen, Lung-chu and Harold D. Lasswell. *Formosa, China and the United Nations.* New York: St. Martin's Press, 1967.
Ching, Leo T.S. *Becoming Japanese: Colonial Taiwan and the Politics of Identity Formation.* Berkeley, CA: University of California Press, 2001.
Communist China 1955–1959 Policy Documents with Analysis. Cambridge, MA: Harvard University Press, 1965.
Eisenhower, Dwight D. *Waging Peace The White House Years; A Personal Account 1956-1961.* Garden City, NY: Doubleday, 1965.
Goddard, W.G. *Formosa A Study in Chinese History.* New York: Macmillan, 1966.
Kerr, George H. *Formosa Licensed Revolution and the Home Rule Movement 1895–1945.* Honolulu: University Press of Hawaii, 1974.
Kissinger, Henry. *Diplomacy.* New York: Simon & Schuster, 1994.
Kuo, Shirley, Gustav Ranis, and John C.H. Fei. (eds.) *The Taiwan Success Story: Rapid Growth with Improved Distribution in the ROC 1952–1979.* Boulder, CO: Westview, 1981.

Lai, Tse-han, Ramon H. Myers, and Wei Wou. *A Tragic Beginning; The Taiwan Uprising of February 28, 1947.* Stanford, CA: Stanford University Press, 1991.
Lilley, James. *China Hands Nine Decades of Adventure, Espionage and Diplomacy in Asia.* New York: Public Affairs, 2004.
Major Problems of United States Foreign Policy 1954. Washington, DC: Brookings Institution, 1954.
Marks, Frederick W. *Power and Peace: The Diplomacy of John Foster Dulles.* Westport, CT: Praeger, 1993.
McGlothlen, Ronald. *Controlling the Waves: Dean Acheson and U.S. Foreign Policy in Asia.* New York: Norton Press, 1993.
Metzler, John J. *Divided Dynamism The Diplomacy of Separated Nations: Germany, Korea, China,* 2nd edition. Lanham, MD: University Press of America, 2014.
Military Balance 1969–1970. London: Institute for Strategic Studies. 1969.
_____. 1979. London: International Institute for Strategic Studies, 1979.
_____. 1997. London: International Institute for Strategic Studies, 1997.
_____. 2015. London: International Institute for Strategic Studies, 2015.
Myers, Ramon H. *Two Societies in Opposition; The Republic of China and the People's Republic of China after Forty Years.* Stanford: Hoover Institution, 1991.
_____. *The Struggle Across the Taiwan Straits/The Divided China Problem.* Stanford, CA: Hoover Institution Press, 2006.
Nixon, Richard. *Beyond Peace.* New York: Random House, 1994.
Paine, S.C.M. *The Sino Japanese War of 1894–1895; Perceptions, Power and Primacy.* Cambridge, UK: Cambridge University Press, 2003.
Rigger, Shelley. *Why Taiwan Matters Small Island, Global Powerhouse,* updated edition. Lanham, MD: Rowman & Littlefield, 2014.
Rubenstein, Murray. (ed.) *Taiwan: A New History.* Armonk, NY: M.E. Sharpe, 1999.
Sih, Paul K.T. (ed.) *Taiwan in Modern Times.* New York: St. John's University, 1973.
Spector, Ronald H. *Eagle Against the Sun; The American War Against Japan.* New York: Free Press, 1985.
Sun, Yat-sen. *San Min Chu I/The Three Principles of the People.* Chungking: Ministry of Information of the Republic of China, 1943.
Yahuda, Michael. *The International Politics of the Asia-Pacific, 1945–1995.* London: Routledge, 1997.

Select Articles

Bellows, Thomas J. Taiwan's Foreign Policy in the 1970's: A Case Study in Adaptation and Viability. Occasional Papers/Reprints Series in Contemporary Asian Studies Number 4, School of Law. University of Maryland, 1977:1–22.

Chen, Qimao. New Approaches in China's Foreign Policy. *Asian Survey* 27(November 1987).
Chao, Chien-min. Xi Jinping's Policies Towards Taiwan After the Nine-in-One Elections. *Prospect Journal* Taiwan Forum 13(April 2015):143–61.
Chien, Frederick. A View from Taipei. *Foreign Affairs* 70(Winter 1991–1992):93–103.
Corcuff, Stephane. Supporters of Unification and the Taiwanization Movement. *China Perspectives* 53(2004):49–65.
Friedberg, Aaron L. The Debate over US China Strategy. *Survival* 57(3) (June–July 2015):89–110.
Harding, Harry. The Concept of a Greater China: Themes, Variations and Reservations. *China Quarterly* 136(December 1993):660–86.
Horowitz, Shale, and Alexander Tan. The Strategic Logic of Taiwanization. *World Affairs* 168(2) (Fall 2005):87–95.
Hu, Weixing. Two State Theory Versus One China Principle: Cross-Straits Relations in 1999. *China Review* (2000):135–56.
Inglehart and Christian Welzel. How Development Leads to Democracy–What We Know About Modernization. *Foreign Affairs* 88(2) (March/April 2009):33–48.
Kim, Seung-young. Russo-Japanese Rivalry over Korean Buffer at the Beginning of the 20th Century and Its Implications. *Diplomacy & Statecraft* 16(4) (2005):619–50.
Metzler, John J. Rejoining the Club: The Republic of China on Taiwan's Bid for United Nations Participation: Prospects and Portents. Presented at the Northeastern Political Science Association, Philadelphia, 17 November 2011.
Sullivan, Jonathan. Taiwan's Identity Crisis. *The National Interest*, 18 August 2014.
Tai, Raymond R.M. The Vatican's Dilemma; Taipei and/or Beijing. Lecture at the International Institute of Asian Studies and the Sinological Institute, Leiden University, the Netherlands, April 25, 2002.

INDEX

A
Acheson, Dean, 34–6, 47
Agency for International Development (AID), 41–4
Allied POW's in Taiwan, 18
American Institute on Taiwan (AIT), 71, 73, 139
Ami, 13, 95
Ando Rikichi, 19, 24
Anti-Secession Law (2005), 102–8, 143
Association for Relations Across the Taiwan Straits (ARATS), 75, 80, 81, 117
Atayal, 95
August Arms Sales Communiqué (1982), 71

B
Ban, Ki-moon, 107
Big Five/WWII Allies, 47, 49, 65
Brzezinski, Zbigniew, 67, 68
Bush, George H.W., 54
Bush, George W., 106, 107
Bush, Richard, 126, 139, 141, 145

C
Cairo Conference (1943), 21
Canadian Trade Office, 73
Carter, Jimmy, 67–8
Chen, Shui-bian, 93–108
Chen, Yi, 15, 23–5, 27, 29, 31, 106
Chiang Ching-kuo, 30, 60, 64, 71, 72, 75
Chiang Kai-shek, 21, 22, 28, 31, 35, 50, 52, 54, 59, 61, 83, 84, 102, 105–6
Chiang Kai-shek *Memorial Hall*, 65, 66, 107, 117, 118
Chien, Frederick, 82
China, 1, 3–9, 13, 15–17, 21, 22, 24–6, 30–6, 39–57, 59–77, 79–91, 93–109, 111–35, 138–47
China Card Policy, 67–9
China Lobby, 51, 52, 57n34

Note: Page number followed by 'n' refers to endnotes.

China Seat United Nations, 47, 49, 53–5
Chinese Communist Party (CCP), 98, 119, 128, 141, 142, 146, 147
Chinese Dream policy, 146
Chou En-lai, 45, 60
Churchill, Winston, 21, 22
Clinton, Bill, 84
Cold War, 30, 39–57, 82, 141, 144
Confucianism, 7, 137
Consensus 1992, 75, 78n42, 80–2, 89, 112, 119, 128, 130, 132
Constitution/ROC, 10, 23–7, 35, 42, 44–8, 50–5, 59, 61, 62, 65, 68, 70, 72, 74–6, 81, 82, 85–90, 96, 98, 99, 102, 103, 105–7, 112–18, 120, 122, 123, 138, 140, 143, 147
Costa Rica, 112, 113
Cousin Lee Cartoon, 72

D
Democratic Progressive Party (DPP), vi, 29, 70, 79–82, 85, 86, 93–102, 104–8, 117, 118, 121, 124, 126, 128–30, 132, 143, 145, 147
Deng Xiaoping, 68, 69, 75, 87, 98
Dewey, George, 9
Diaoyutai/Senkaku Islands, 122, 123, 147
Diplomatic relations/isolation, 60, 65, 67–9, 76, 81
Double Ten Day, 118
Dulles, John Foster, 36, 46–7, 50

E
East China Sea Peace Initiative, 134n31
Economic Cooperation Framework Agreement (ECFA), 115–17

Eisenhower, Dwight D., 43, 45, 46, 50, 57, 65
Executive Yuan, 61, 124
Export Processing Zone (EPZ), 64

F
February 28 Incident 1947, 27–32
Finlandization, 144, 145
Ford Administration, 67
Formosa/*aka* Taiwan, 3, 5–19, 20n38, 21–3, 25, 26, 28–32, 34–7, 39–41, 46, 48, 50, 51, 69, 95, 122, 132
Formosa Resolution 1955, 46
Freedom House, 138

G
Geneva Peace Conference 1954, 45
Germany, 2, 5, 9, 73, 90
Ghali, Boutros Boutros, 82
Greater China concept, 138, 145, 146
Green Tech, 127–8
Guangxu, *Emperor*, 6

H
Haig, Alexander, 70, 78n29
Hasegawa, Kiyoshi, 17, 19
Hirohito, *Emperor*, 15
Hokkien/Taiwanese language, 84, 86
Hong Kong Handover 1997, 87, 88
Hsinchu Science Park, 127
Hu Jintao, 103, 106
Hungary, 48, 49
Hyperinflation, 33

I
Inchon Landings 1950, 40
Indigenous Peoples/*Austronesian* peoples, 95

International Civil Aviation Organization (ICAO), 55, 114, 115
International Cooperation and Development Fund (ICDF)
Isla Formosa, 1, 6
Israel, 72, 120
Italy, 49, 59
Ito Hirobumi, 4, 5

J
Jacoby, Neil, 43–5, 52, 56n12
Japan, 1–6, 8, 9, 11, 12, 14–17, 22, 23, 28, 35, 36, 39, 40, 43, 53, 59, 74, 84, 88, 113, 114, 121, 123, 126, 138, 144–6
 colonial rule over Taiwan, 42
Jiang Zemin, 88, 98
Judd, Walter, 51
Judicial Yuan, 62

K
Kaohsiung, 28, 64, 69, 84, 104, 118, 126, 155
Kaohsiung *Incident*, 70
Keelung, 1, 6–8, 11, 17, 18, 24, 27, 28, 64, 84, 122
Kerr, George, 7, 9–11, 15, 16, 30–2, 101
Kissinger, Henry, 60, 67, 70
Kodama, Gentaro, 10, 11
Kominka, 15, 16
Koo, C. F., 81
Korean War 1950–53, 36, 37, 39, 40, 47
Kuomintang/Nationalist Party (KMT), 23, 24, 28–31, 35, 39, 41, 51–2, 61, 65, 69, 70, 74, 75, 79–82, 84–6, 88, 93, 94, 96, 99–101, 103–7, 111–13, 118, 123, 126, 128, 129, 132, 145, 147

L
Land reform, 41–3, 51, 61, 66
Land to the Tiller Program, 42, 43, 61
Lee Teng-hui, 84–6, 89, 90, 98, 100, 105, 141
Legislative Yuan, 62, 84, 123, 129
Li, Hung-chang, 4, 5
Li, Peng, 85
Lien, Chan, 85, 88, 93, 100, 103, 146
Lilley, James, 68, 70, 71
Lu, Annette, 99, 100

M
Ma, Ying-jeou, 111, 112, 123, 126, 128, 129, 140, 141
MacArthur, Douglas, 18–19, 39, 40, 55n3
Mainland Affairs Council (MAC), 80, 81, 88, 121, 130
Mainland Flights/Tourism, 117
Mainland Trade, 80, 130
Manchuria/*Manchukuo*, 16, 22, 26, 34
Mandarin/language, 23, 25, 61, 84, 87, 118
Mao Tse-tung, 25, 26, 31, 33, 35, 36, 47, 60, 66
Marshall, George, 26
Martial Law Lifted 1987, 30, 75
Meiji Restoration/*Period*, 2, 10

N
Nationalist Party/aka KMT, 23, 24, 28–31, 35, 39, 41, 51–2, 61, 65, 69, 70, 74, 75, 79–82, 84–6, 88, 93, 94, 96, 99–101, 103–7, 111–13, 118, 123, 126, 128, 129, 132, 145, 147
National Palace Museum, v, 117
National Peoples Congress (NPC), 69, 102, 103

New Party, 80, 85, 100
Nicaragua, 82
Nitobe Inazo, 9–11
Nixon, Richard M., 50, 53, 55, 59, 60, 66–8, 98
  Nixon Shock, 53, 57n39
  Visit to China 1972, 59

O
Obama, Barack, 144
One country, two systems, 69, 87, 88, 144
Oolong tea, 7, 15
Opium War, 1

P
Pacific Pivot, 144, 147
Panama, 11, 112, 115
Pan Blue, 94, 100, 101, 104, 147
Pan Green, 101, 104, 147
Pearl Harbor, 17, 18
Peng, Meng-chi, 28
People's Republic of China (PRC), vi, 45, 48, 49, 52–4, 60, 65, 67–72, 74–6, 80–5, 87–90, 93, 94, 97–100, 102–4, 106, 112, 113, 115–17, 119–21, 123, 124, 126, 128, 129, 132, 138–47
Perry, Matthew, 1, 6
Pescadores Islands, *Penghu*, 1, 6, 22, 46
Pew Poll, 142

Q
Qian, Qichen, 83
Qing Dynasty, 2, 6, 7, 12, 23, 124

Quemoy/*Kinmen*, 45, 46, 50–1

R
Reagan, Ronald, 70, 71, 74
Religions, 16, 137
Republic of China/Taiwan, vi, 21, 22, 26, 41, 45–9, 51–4, 59–91, 93–135, 138, 139, 142, 143, 146
Retrocession/1945, 22, 23, 25, 26
Rockefeller, Nelson, 65
Rogers, William, 53, 123
Roosevelt, Franklin D., 18, 21
Rusk, Dean, 35, 36, 41

S
San Min Chu I/Three Principles of the People, 13, 62
Seventh Fleet, 40, 41
Shanghai Communiqué 1972, 59, 60
Shimonoseki Treaty 1895, 5, 6, 8, 9, 122
Singapore, 81, 121, 127, 128, 137, 138, 145
Sino-Japanese War, 4
Soong, James, 93, 100, 102, 129, 146
Soviet Union, 47, 66, 67, 70, 82, 99, 144
St. Vincent and the Grenadines, 115
Straits Exchange Foundation (SEF), 75, 80, 81, 89, 117, 130, 133
Stuart, John Leighton, 31–3
Su Chi, 75, 81
Sunflower Movement, 123, 124
Sun Li-jen, 35

Sun Yat-sen, 12, 13, 23, 50, 61, 62, 65, 66, 101, 112, 118, 119, 124

T
Taipei 101, vi, 66, 171
Taipei Economic and Cultural Office (TECO), 150
Taiwan
  diplomatic isolation, 60, 76, 81
  economic miracle, 74, 124
  separatism and independence, 94, 120, 129–30, 143
  Taiwanization, 74, 79, 85, 95, 96, 101, 102, 108, 147
Taiwan Relations Act (TRA) 1979, 68, 71, 87, 131, 143, 144
Tang Ching-sung, 8
Teng, Teresa, 72
Ten Major Projects, 64
Tokugawa *shogunate*, 1
Triple Intervention, 5
Truman, Harry, 26, 31, 34–6, 40
Tsai, Ing-wen, 128–32
Typhoon *Morakot*, 113

U
Unification, 88, 98, 102, 105, 106, 121, 122, 146
United Nations
  China Seat dispute, 47, 53–5, 82
  Taiwan/ROC moves to regain membership, 44, 99
United States, 12, 33, 35, 39, 41, 42, 46, 48, 49, 55, 59, 85, 87, 98, 114, 119, 120, 131, 139, 141, 144

V
Vietnam, 45, 49, 53, 60, 66, 69, 121, 139, 146

W
Waishengren/Mainlanders, 23, 25, 27, 29, 86, 95, 96, 105, 106
Wei, Tao-ming, 31
White Terror, 29, 30, 93
World Health Organization (WHO), 55, 114, 115
  Taiwan Observer Status, 114

X
Xi, Jinping, 119, 121, 128, 146, 147

Y
Yahuda, Michael, 60, 67
Yeh, George K. C., 46

Z
Zhou Enlai, 60